Grit, Grime and Glory

Discovering Jesus in the Pains and Mysteries of Life

Dave Price

Jesus Movement Publishing

Copyright © 2023 by Dave Price

All rights reserved. No portion of this book may be reproduced in any form without written permission from the publisher or author, except as permitted by U.S. copyright law.

Cover image © Paul Kellet

All Scripture quotations, unless otherwise indicated, are taken from the Holy Bible, New International Version®, NIV®. Copyright ©1973, 1978, 1984, 2011 by Biblica, Inc.™ Used by permission of Zondervan. All rights reserved worldwide. www.zondervan.com The "NIV" and "New International Version" are trademarks registered in the United States Patent and Trademark Office by Biblica, Inc.™

Published by Jesus Movement Publishing 2023

ISBN: 978-1-7384555-0-8

e-ISBN: 978-1-7384555-1-5

Recommendations

As I've read Dave's book I've been reminded afresh that the life of a disciple is a journey. Sometimes that journey can be fun and filled with amazing things and sometimes the journey takes turns we'd really rather it didn't. One of the joys of the journey of a disciple is knowing that at every step, whether easy or hard, God is with us and His promise is to lead us along the path of life. He really does lead us on some adventurous ways. Another joy of the journey is that we get to travel together. I have had the joy of travelling with Dave through many of the stories in this book. Many times we have spent time talking, reflecting, asking, learning, growing and many times we have been awestruck by what God has done. Dave is passionate about the journey of discipleship. He loves to listen and learn and grow from what he is journeying through. As you read you will realise that he loves to be a disciple that passes his learnings from the journey on to other disciples. He is passionate about being a disciple and making disciples. I love journeying with my friend Dave. As you journey through this book with him, I hope and pray you are helped along the discipleship journey.

Andy Cooley

Church Engagement Message Trust

Dave's book is a powerful story of a raw, authentic journey of discipleship. His remarkable honesty captivates and inspires, offering a compelling narrative that resonates deeply with anyone yearning for more in life. Through his experiences, Dave demonstrates a real dedication to mission and an passionate commitment to seeking out people far from God. A must-read for those seeking to follow Christ in today's world.

Simon Holley

Senior Leader, Catalyst Network

I've known Dave for at least thirty years and have seen first hand some of the experiences laid out so clearly and vulnerably in his book. Dave makes it clear to all in practical ways how an ordinary life can perform extraordinary things for God. Many books unintentionally take the high ground showing through their pages that they have arrived or succeeded. Dave's account shows clearly that he has been in the valley where many of us spend a large part of our lives.

Stewart Johnson

Leadership Team at the Community Church, Wooburn Green, UK

This book you are about to read is one that will take you on a journey as you delve into the reality of what it looks like to live as a true disciple of Jesus. As Dave very vulnerably exposes throughout these pages, this not only looks like mountaintop experiences, for a true disciple must yield fully to the call of God regardless of where that might lead us. These pages are full of lived experience and the lessons Dave has chosen to learn through them. His passion and commitment to his beliefs are the strength to this story. Holding nothing back he helpfully shares the tools he has found useful and encourages us to 'make disciples, not converts'

RECOMMENDATIONS

take risks and above all love God in a way that sees His Glory revealed to those around us. You will be encouraged indeed!

Kerensa McCulloch

Freelancer

Grit Grime and Glory is a authentic, informed, and powerful read. It is a testament to the knowledge and pragmatic faith that Dave Price possesses, it is the type of book that I believe the culture needs, particularly for those who have questions about their faith or facing difficulties in believing. I recommend this book for the mature Christians as well as the new Christian. It particularly blessed and encouraged me as an artist in the entertainment industry to continue to conduct myself as an apprentice of Jesus, and as someone of Christ like power and character rather than a surface level faith. Exceptional book

NamesBliss

Grime Artist

I love this book. It is refreshingly honest as Dave describes his particular journey of faith. It is not a "how to" book with solutions for every situations but it is a book that inspires the reader to work out their own application of faith. This is a book that church leaders can use in abundance to give to anyone on a journey of faith but particularly to those who are at the beginning of a search for God. I recommend this wonderful book to anyone on a journey of faith no matter at what stage they might be.

Dr Rev'd Martin Robinson

FCC National Leader

I'm happy to recommend this book to you because I am happy to recommend the man who wrote it! Dave is one of life's good guys. He has a rare passion for God and people and a willingness to obey God even when it hurts to do so. You will love the authenticity, provocation and encouragement contained in this book. I pray it causes you to run after Jesus with fresh fire and fresh gratitude.

Phil Wilthew

Catalyst Hub Leader

Dave Price carries an Apostolic gifting to see the kingdom of God revealed on the earth where it is currently very hard ground. There is a cost to being a pioneer and Dave is willing to risk it all for Jesus. Dave has been one of the most influential and inspirational leaders I know. He is willing to go and make disciples and also carry his cross. Dave sees the now word of God before it is reality and the rest catch up.

David Bennett

Account Executive

Contents

Acknowledgements	IX
Foreword	XI

Chapter

1. Introduction — 1

Part 1 - Grit:

2. My Story: No Turning Back — 11
3. Reclaiming Faith — 21
4. Where Is the Power? — 35
5. Did I Hear Right? — 45

Part 2 - Grime:

6. Why, God? — 61
7. Hitting the Wall — 71
8. Tools for Healthy Emotions and Spiritual Well-Being — 87

Part 3 - Glory:

9. Mountains and Valleys — 103
10. Making God Known — 115
11. Kingdom Jigsaw — 125

Acknowledgements

Thank you to my amazing wife Kaz, you've been such a huge blessing and constant support. To Ariella, Theo and Selah who make our lives' so much fuller while we all seek to follow God's plans for us as a family.

Thanks to my mum and late father who have championed and prayed for me every step of the way especially when I went rogue for many years.

Thank you, PK (artwork), Simon (formatting) and Jesse (editor) – what a team you've been behind this project bringing it to life.

Thank you to Trinity Church, London, The Community Church, Wooburn Green and Rowheath Pavilion Church, Birmingham. You have each been and are a huge part of my story.

Thank you to all my Catalyst & Resonate friends especially Andy R and PJ. You helped to bring me back from some dark places many times.

Finally, Father, Jesus and Holy Spirit, my life is Yours. Thank You for Your constant love and grace.

Dave Price

Foreword

I HAVE HAD THE privilege of knowing Dave over many years in various capacities. Initially, it was somewhat formal as part of my role in the Catalyst network of churches in Newfrontiers, where I was assisting the churches in both London and Woburn Green where Dave was in Leadership. Over time, even though I am ?? years his senior, we became good friends and have enjoyed "doing life" together regardless of those formal structures. This was just as well as eventually I ended up moving from the Catalyst Network to another part of Newfrontiers and ultimately Dave left Newfrontiers altogether.

Whilst it may be assumed that, as the older man, I was disciplining Dave, the truth is that genuine discipleship is a two-way street as we both look to be apprentices of Jesus. Yes, I have seen more of life than Dave and am more like a father than a peer, but his life, as you will read in this book, has given him a unique perspective, understanding and insight that I have to say has helped, inspired and encouraged me to be a more authentic disciple and apprentice of Jesus myself.

In the messiness of life, we have battled depression together, I have walked Dave through some particularly dark times in his life, and latterly he has walked alongside me as I battle cancer. I believe this is the discipleship Dave talks about and Jesus modelled, where in the providence of

God, both parties are mutually encouraged, strengthened, and inspired to keep following Jesus through the grit, grime, and glory of life!

I have known Dave long enough, walked with him far enough, and know him deep enough to tell you that what you read in this book is authentically Dave! There is nothing theoretical about the things he talks about in this book. Yes, there is theological depth and a strong biblical basis to support his claims, but more importantly, there is a wealth of examples and experiences that will inspire you, as he has me, to walk the talk, be more like Jesus, do the things Jesus did and expect the miraculous as we walk through the mundane.

Andy Robinson

Christ Central Apostolic Team

Chapter 1

Introduction

For many years, I've considered writing a book about what I've learnt as a disciple of Jesus—from the everyday practices of prayer, Bible study, worship, service, Sabbath (a day of rest), church life, and sharing the Gospel, to the more 'charismatic' or 'supernatural' activity that can occur when a disciple of Jesus is filled with the Holy Spirit. The latter includes healings, miracles, outrageous generosity, mind-boggling visions, or even prophecies that make you think someone has bugged your house because they seem to know so much about you.

But these extraordinary moments are not what being a disciple is. Being a disciple is believing and leaning into Jesus Christ in every moment, even the mundane ones—and especially the painful and mysterious ones. In that way, my story is anything but extraordinary. It's grimy. It's messy. My journey to loving God has not been a straight line but one of trying, failing, taking risks, hurting people, being hurt by people, praising in one moment and sinning in the next, experiencing rejection, and often asking, "Why, God?"

This book is designed to lift the lid on the reality of being a disciple of Jesus and welcome you into moments of learning, heartache, extraordinary pain, and ridiculous glory as God breaks into those human experiences we all have. The heart of this book is honesty about the struggles so many people experience in their lives, and it will perhaps introduce you to a more authentic faith in Jesus than what you've seen or heard before.

The Power of the Everyday

Millions of us are scrolling through feeds and posts every day. Sometimes we are laughing at the latest funny viral post. Other times we're looking for answers to some of life's bigger questions. Why am I here? What is life about? How can I find peace instead of anxiety? Is this it? What happens when we die? How can I make sense of suffering and pain? Why are there so many religions? Why can't I free myself from this addiction or behaviour? The questions we ask ourselves go on and on, just like our scrolling habits.

Over the last two decades of following Jesus's teaching, I've had to learn to value the everyday, ordinary moments of life. In the same way, I've learnt to practice what some people call 'long obedience'. This idea is not going to go viral anytime soon, but it does provide hope and answers to many of life's major questions.

Advances in technology have hardwired us to want things instantly. We want fast food, drive-thru coffee, a personal transformation from a sixty-second TikTok video—but this isn't really the way of Jesus. Jesus's parable (a story with meaning) of the mustard seed (Matthew 13:31–32) shows the power of the everyday, of incremental growth over years or even decades, which then enables incredible blessings to flow into your life and into the lives of others. In the stories of Jesus, there are moments of instantaneous transformation that we might call 'miracles', but the idea of slow, steady growth or transformation over a lifetime must not be forgotten. There is power in the simple act of following Jesus day by day and being faithful. Over the years, though, I have become increasingly convinced that the more 'boring' practices of Jesus—rest, silence, solitude, prayer, reflection, study, fasting, and fellowship—are the disciplines that lead to a lifestyle of healing, prophetic revelation, power, and dealing with demonic spirits. I don't believe that practising the everyday 'boring' activities of Jesus earns us acceptance with God, merit, or the power to command the more 'miraculous' activities of Jesus. That would be opposite to the teachings of grace found in the Scriptures.[1]

What I do believe is that these ordinary practices create in us a capacity to handle God's blessing in our lives and bless others as well. It's like training our bodies to run a marathon. After working to increase our mileage, we'll be able to complete those gruelling twenty-six miles because we'll have the capacity and the grit to do it. If done consistently, these spiritual practices equip us to do the things Jesus did—not because we earned them, but because we have the capacity to sustain God's blessings in our lives, which overflow to others.

When one grows their awareness of each passing moment and becomes elated when God shows up, they discover that God is always there. It really is amazing when you see God do something incredible with an ordinary moment of your life. We often never know what the power of a text message, kind word, or simple act of generosity will do. As Paul says, "I planted the seed, Apollos watered it, but God has been making it grow" (1 Corinthians 3:6). We simply do not know what faithful, everyday

---

1. Grace in this context is undeserved favour, such as someone giving a stranger a present. The stranger has not earned the present through hard work or some other qualifications. The stranger was given the present simply because the one giving the gift wanted to. This is how God treats us. He freely gives us gifts and offers us forgiveness because He can and wants to.

moments will do. We plant and we water, but God himself brings forth the growth.

God can do all things, and He wastes nothing in our lives. Every story in this book—such as a cigarette purchase leading a man to find God, a flight to India with a stranger, an offer to give a girl a lift to work, and wrestling with burnout and mental health—flows from trying to simply be obedient to Jesus in my everyday moments. Anyone can obey Jesus's guidance, and I invite you to share in my stories of obedience and disobedience, my highs and lows. Hopefully I'll inspire you to see what God might do in your life.

Maybe my story will help you rediscover a faith you've rejected. Others might be encouraged to keep believing despite the difficulties you are facing. For others, this book might be more of an introduction to a life of faith in Jesus and what it really looks like, rather than some cookie-cutter TV version of Jesus and Christianity. I have learnt that God is good and can be trusted, even in the darkest, grimiest moments of my life.

God has taught me so much about myself and others, and it's clear to me that the Father is building His Kingdom much like we might build a jigsaw puzzle. The Father knows what the finished image will look like. He will move and interlock pieces, slowly revealing His glorious Kingdom, until the magnificent day Jesus returns and the fullness of the Kingdom of Heaven is made known to all creation!

In the Gospels, Jesus refers to Heaven and the Kingdom of God in a variety of ways: seed, yeast, virgins, trees, a pearl, and more.[2] Each story

---

2. The Gospels are the first four books of the New Testament and give four different accounts of Jesus's life and ministry.

reveals a facet of the way the Kingdom of God works, and it's up to us as disciples (followers of Jesus's way) to understand the principles Jesus teaches through parables (stories with instruction). As Jesus's disciples, we get to walk with him every day. As we look back at our discipleship journeys, it's easy to see that the Kingdom of God reveals itself in ways both big and small. It can be fast, with dramatic breakthroughs, or slow, which requires enduring faith (or even long suffering). Sometimes its impact is known, and other times we'll only get to hear about it in Heaven. Isn't that beautiful?

The Father reveals and establishes this amazing Kingdom as He works both in us and through us by the power of the Holy Spirit, each day moving and interlocking different pieces of the Kingdom jigsaw puzzle until all the earth is filled with the knowledge of the glory of the Lord (Habakkuk 2:14). The puzzle has billions of pieces, and it's possible that some of them_ _ _ _ ??

This book is designed to help you engage with Jesus and develop your discipleship (apprenticeship) of his ways through His teachings in the Bible and the Holy Spirit, who reminds us of them every day. My prayer is that the lessons, testimonies, and stories that I share will enable you to partner with the Father, Jesus, and the Holy Spirit to place your pieces into this incredible Kingdom jigsaw puzzle.

God has an incredible adventure in store for you. When coupled with everyday faithfulness and devotion to Him, this adventure will lead you to a place of awe and wonder as the glory of God is revealed in you and through you. Just as Jesus promised His disciples, "I have given them the glory You gave Me, so that they may be one as We are one—I in them and You in Me—that they may be perfectly united, so that the world may know that You sent Me and have loved them just as You have loved Me" (John 17:22–23).

Prayer

Jesus, as I read this book, I pray that you speak to me and help me to discover a genuine and authentic faith that has the power to bring transformation and healing into my life. Jesus, I want to know that you are real and that you can be trusted.

Amen.

PART 1 - GRIT.

jm

JESUS MOVEMENT PUBLISHING

Chapter 2

My Story: No Turning Back

I REMEMBER COMING UP the escalator, hundreds of twinkling lights hanging above it. As a kid, it seemed like such a magical place. I was blessed to have parents who loved Jesus. Every Sunday we'd go to church in a cinema in Slough, where we lived at the time. Going to a cinema and exploring all the different parts of the building was such a fun experience as a five-year-old. I'm pretty sure I went into every screen and room and up every lift and staircase I could find.

One of my clearest memories of those Sunday mornings is not of a time of worship or a teaching moment in kid's church, but of watching my dad and another man pray for a man who was on the floor, kicking and screaming. The man on the floor seemed really angry and in a great deal of anguish. From my young viewpoint, it looked to me as if he had a big bubble of snot coming out of his nose. There was some sort of black thing inside it: something like a cartoon devil. As my dad and his friend prayed, the man continued wailing and banging the floor. Suddenly, the snot bubble popped, and he became calm. I didn't know it then, but that was the first time I saw someone freed from a demonic spirit.

We see Jesus helping people who are a danger to themselves and others more frequently in the Gospels than we might imagine happens every day. In one encounter, such an individual has been put in chains by the citizens of the town. When Jesus meets this man, the evil spirits—which call themselves *legion*, meaning 'many'—reveal themselves. Jesus sends them into some pigs, which then run off a cliff![1]

Many years after the incident at the cinema, my sister and I were talking about what happened. In her memory of the event, green smoke came out of the man while he was being prayed for. What I find fascinating about this story is that whilst we both watched the same story play out, we perceived it differently. The end of the story is even more amazing. After I gave my elder brother the manuscript of this book to read, he told me the guy on the floor had gone to Boys' Brigade (a type of youth group) with him. Many years later, they met again at another local church, and he was following Jesus!

That experience has become one of the defining moments of my faith in God. It made me aware of the world beyond what can be seen with our natural eyes—a spiritual world. I imagine it was very transformative for the man too.

From about the age of six onwards, I began to get mocked for my faith in Jesus. My friends at school found it funny to make jokes about the

---

1. "And when He came to the other side into the country of the Gadarenes, two demon-possessed men confronted Him as they were coming out of the tombs. They were so extremely violent that no one could pass by that way. And they cried out, saying, 'What business do You have with us, Son of God? Have You come here to torment us before the time?' Now there was a herd of many pigs feeding at a distance from them. And the demons begged Him, saying, 'If You are going to cast us out, send us into the herd of pigs.' And He said to them, 'Go!' And they came out and went into the pigs; and behold, the whole herd rushed down the steep bank into the sea and drowned in the waters." (Matthew 8:28–33)

worship songs my parents listened to in the car on the way to football. There was a show called *Father Ted* on TV at the time, and I was nicknamed Father Dave. This ridicule, coupled with the fact that I didn't feel that I fit in at the church we'd moved to, led me to lose my love for the church. I felt like an outsider. I'm sure many of you can relate. At that time in my life, that sense of not being welcome or not fitting in came from the perception that we lived in the wrong area and that I was a bit rough around the edges, so to speak. Plus, some of the other parents in the church had made some unhelpful comments about me to my parents.

By the age of eleven, I found myself believing in Jesus but despising the church. Years of my parents reading the Bible to me and praying for me had convinced me God was real, but I found the church to be irrelevant to my life. I was rejected by those within it and ridiculed by my friends outside it. It's a strange sensation to feel you don't fit in. I'm sure you can relate in some way. Maybe it's at work, in your family, at church, or in some team you are a part of.

This feeling became a deadly combination. I sought acceptance elsewhere, leading me into a lifestyle that was antichurch and against the teachings of Jesus. I became increasingly focused on doing things the Bible said not to. By my late teens, I was living a wild and ungodly life; you name it, I did it. I wasn't just living my life unaware of God and his ways; I was intentionally doing the opposite of what I knew God wanted for my life. I felt rejected by the church and therefore by God, so I rejected them in turn.

When I'm talking to people about Jesus and faith, something that comes up often is the idea that a person is not good enough for God because of all the 'stuff' they've done. However, the Bible teaches us that we will never be good enough for God. In fact, it teaches us that "while we were enemies of God, Jesus died for our sins" (Romans 5:10). This means we can never mess up beyond what God is willing to forgive. I've found this to be true. Despite everything I've done, God loves and accepts me. I may have rejected the church, the church might have rejected me, but God loves and accepts me as I am.

Experiencing God's acceptance has been incredibly healing. If you've experienced rejection and the heartache that goes with it, I want to remind you that Jesus died on a cross for you. God loves and accepts you, regardless of your past, present, or even your future. My prayer for you, as you read this sentence, is that you experience God's love, acceptance, and affirmation right now. Jesus is for you and loves you beyond measure.

I was in my late teens when my world began to crash. My girlfriend at the time had become pregnant; she was already three months along when we found out. Logically, an abortion seemed like the best option for us, but emotionally neither of us was convinced this was the right decision.

I now recognise that this is when God began to intervene in my life. We decided to go through with the abortion. I remember the nurse doing an ultrasound scan and showing us the image of this twenty-some-thing-week-old baby before the procedure started. I was asked to leave the room while the procedure took place. With the image of this precious child imprinted on my mind, I, overwhelmed by shame and self-hatred, went to the car and got super high to deal with the turmoil. As you might have guessed, our relationship didn't last much longer. We were broken people, and this process created a deep void in me.

My heart grew cold to protect it from the pain and shame I felt. This was one of the darkest and grimiest moments of my life. Looking back, I wonder if I simply shut down emotionally so I could move on with my life. I filled this void with all kinds of wild living, but it was never enough. My sister later told me I'd called her 'off my head' asking, "If God could forgive a murderer, could God forgive me?" I was looking for a change but wasn't sure what changes to make. Forgetting the pain of what I'd done was my way of life.

I'd hit rock bottom. I hated who I'd become and was failing at college too. But slowly God was breaking into my life—I just didn't know it yet. God is so kind, and His grace is so amazing that He somehow uses our detours, failings, and brokenness to lead us back to the right path, even if it takes years. His patience with our mistakes and bad ideas is astonishing.

One day, my Business Studies teacher asked me to stay behind after the lesson. She told me that she'd help me pass my exams if I did an extra lesson with her on Friday afternoon. Something inside me decided that I would turn up. Considering my attendance was less than 50 percent, this was a miracle. Looking back, I can see Jesus beginning to help me turn my life around. True to her word, this teacher taught me the skills I needed to pass my exams, and my grades went up dramatically, giving me the opportunity to apply for university.

Around the same time, my friend who picked up drugs from our dealer lost his driving licence after being pulled over for drinking and driving. This created an opportunity for me to stop using drugs and dealing, which was a battle I'd been trying to win for a while.

I was looking to make some positive changes in my life. My sister had started going to church in London and asked if I'd take her. Going back to church felt like a huge step after so many years, but something in my spirit said yes again. I began going with her regularly. Once again, although I didn't know it at the time, Jesus was transforming my life from the inside out.

By the summer of that year, I'd passed my A-levels, had a university offer, and wasn't using drugs. There was a long, gritty journey ahead of me, but the combination of an abortion, the kindness of my teacher, a friend losing his driving licence, the decision to stop using and dealing drugs, and attending a church that felt relevant to my life had caused the brilliance of God's glory to break in and push back the darkness that had taken over.

Over the summer, I kept going to church and slowly began to rebuild my relationship with Jesus. In September 2003, I started university. For the first few weeks, things were going okay, but old habits crept back in. Perhaps you can relate to this: you really want to do the right thing or make a change, but somehow end up doing the very thing you're trying to stop. I had one foot in the world and one foot in the church. But no one could keep doing the splits forever, and I ended up back doing all the things that had caused me so much pain, shame, and heartache.

Going into my final year at university, I was determined to demonstrate some grit and endurance. Over the summer, I had been away at a young adult camp, met some awesome people, and was introduced to some Christian rap artists I really liked. Lecrae had just dropped his first album, *Real Talk*, and Flame's bars were amazing. Discovering music I enjoyed and that fit with my life experiences and culture helped me with my journey of faith. In the rhymes and beats, I found acceptance of shared experiences and discovered how the Gospel could bring healing and deliverance. In this music, I found a place I could call home. Jesus was now present in my life through the music I was listening to, and through the music's reliance on the Word of God, I began to read the Bible once again.

My outward life was still rather messy, but my internal world was finding strength, comfort, and peace in God. Each weekend, I travelled up from Chichester to London to serve at church on Sunday before heading back to uni again. By the end of my final year, I was a first-class student, having drastically pulled my grades up from the two previous years, and was a devoted follower of Jesus. There was no turning back for me. I'd done so much of what the world calls fun. I had the T-shirt, the scars, and the photos I hope never make it to social media. But God had broken into my life, pushed back the darkness, and given me a new life. I knew this was it. No compromise. No turning back. I needed to embrace a life spent following Jesus.

Whatever your story, it's your story—and it's powerful. I know God is at work in your life, either awakening you to his love and ways or leading you down the proper path. We can never go beyond God's ability to restore and redeem, no matter what we've done or had done to us. God's grace knows no bounds or limits. As the Scriptures say, "His grace is sufficient" (2 Corinthians 12:9).

I'm sure God would prefer it if we took the straight and narrow path Jesus so beautifully modelled. Luckily for us, God knows we are but dust (Psalm 103:14), and in His brilliance He works through all of our detours, shortcomings, and even blatant rebellion. It's never too late for us to turn to God, seek forgiveness, and discover His mercy really is new every morning. His grace truly is amazing.

Prayer

Thank you, Jesus. Although I may have given up on you, you have never given up on me. In spite of my failings, you still love me and have good plans and desires for my life. Today I confess my sin and faithlessness. Fill me with your love and grace, and guide me to the right path: God's path. Amen

Chapter 3

Reclaiming Faith

When you hear the word *teacher*, what comes to mind? A schoolteacher? A college or University lecturer? A church pastor? Do you think about information and how it can be shared or received? Do you think of tradespersons or creatives, such as electricians, plumbers, painters, and sculptors? One who teaches not so much through information but through modelling and demonstration?

In the West, most of our learning is structured around;

1. Receiving information, often in a classroom setting.

2. A theoretical environment where we don't receive real-life or hands-on experience.

Consequently, discipleship or instruction in Christianity has been based on acquiring and understanding knowledge, not practising the ways of Jesus in real life. In my journey with Jesus, I've longed for people of faith to walk alongside me and show me how to live life in our modern day while still using Jesus's values as my foundation—to walk alongside me in the grit and grime of everyday life and show me a more glorious way. I wonder if you can relate to this desire. We all want to look up to someone who doesn't just say the right things but actually puts them into practise in their life. To be a genuine role model.

There are endless challenges in life, and a thirty-minute sermon is rarely the answer. However, to have someone show you the ropes and teach you how to overcome or faithfully endure these challenges is an incredible blessing. This is exactly what Jesus did for his disciples, what the apostle Paul did for Timothy, and what Jesus wants us to experience. Living our everyday lives with an authentic faith fills us with hope, love, and peace, even in the grimiest moments.

Jesus lived, slept, ate, walked, talked, and demonstrated true Christianity to his disciples. It was personal and real. Jesus went to parties and funerals, walked the streets, engaged with people of every social group, travelled from villages to towns to cities, and was rejected by some and loved by others. Jesus lived out his faith in His Father and partnership with the Holy Spirit in all kinds of settings, modelling right behaviour and teaching his disciples as he went. This approach to teaching is far more reminiscent of a tradesperson teaching an apprentice rather than a schoolteacher teaching a student. It's this varied, life-on-life approach that leads to a genuine transformative discipleship experience. Jesus's desire for us isn't that we attend a church service once a week and listen to a message from the pastor, but that we be equipped through a life-on-life role-modelling type of apprenticeship. This is the way of Jesus, and it's far better than the disconnected model many Christians have experienced.

Church should be less like going to the theatre or a lecture and far more like going to work with a tradesperson and learning new skills every day. I often meet people who are frustrated by church in one way or another, and many of us are carrying some pain from our experiences with these organisations. I believe Jesus is inviting us to rethink church—specifically our understanding of discipleship.

If you've been attending church for some time now, I'm sure you've noticed that increased theological knowledge often seems to be the end goal. To be a disciple of Jesus, it seems we must know more! And if things aren't quite making sense in our lives, we clearly don't know enough. This is the model of Christian discipleship I'm sure most of us have experienced. But what happens when we really examine the Gospels and look at how Jesus taught his followers?

Did Jesus teach his disciples like a schoolteacher, passing on information? Or was he like a tradesperson, modelling a way of doing things? Do we find Jesus having theoretical conversation in a sterile environment?

No, we find Jesus debating with religious leaders, modelling how to properly deal with conflict. We find Jesus using everyday life experiences to teach and equip his disciples. At a dinner, one lady (probably a prostitute) anoints Jesus's feet. He uses this moment to talk about sin and love (Luke 7:36–50). There are many people present, and Jesus uses this moment as an object lesson for all present, which includes the woman, the disciples, the religious leaders of the day, and those serving the table.

Jesus's primary teaching method was modelling the will of God the Father to his disciples in everyday moments. "The reason the Son of God appeared was to destroy the devil's work" (1 John 3:8). He did this in the everyday. Jesus wants to walk alongside you there so you can have an authentic faith.

Unfortunately, too many of us have dealt with hypocritical church pastors who say one thing and do another. We might have been made to feel deeply inadequate or shamed by someone in church leadership, only to later discover that their lives are just as messy as ours. Maybe we've become aware of another scandal of some nature. These kinds of negative experiences can often leave us feeling confused and disappointed with the church and Christianity at large. However, Jesus is not a hypocrite, and there is no hidden scandal with Him. Therefore, we'd do well to shift our focus away from church pastors and back to Jesus, the true teacher of our faith.

The world is desperate to see the real Jesus and his love, grace, mercy, and justice. Yet all too often, we encounter people who claim to follow Jesus and have biblical beliefs but not biblical ways of living. There's an old album called *Jesus Freak* by DC Talk, and the beginning of one of the tracks has a skit that goes, "The greatest single cause of atheism in the world today is Christians who acknowledge Jesus with their lips and walk out the door and deny him by their lifestyle. That is what an unbelieving world simply finds unbelievable."

Even as a child, I was aware of this dynamic, and I'm guessing you are familiar with it too.

There is a better way, though. When we reclaim our faith and build solely on daily life with Jesus, we are positioning ourselves to be transformed. We begin a journey of authentic faith, discipleship, and exploration with Jesus, where a change in our beliefs and behaviours happens.

Learning from Jesus

Jesus trained his disciples to value what he valued and demonstrate those values daily. Jesus equipped them with the right beliefs and behaviours by modelling those beliefs and behaviours himself. Jesus empowered his disciples and wants us to do the same.

In the first chapter of the Gospel of Mark, Jesus invites some of those following him to be disciples of his teachings. By chapter 6, they've seen Jesus miraculously heal people, pray by himself, eat with those the religious leaders called sinners, teach about demonic powers, redefine the religious community's understanding of the Sabbath, preach in accessible ways that use everyday analogies, and supernaturally calm a storm. If that wasn't enough, they go on to witness him restore a man oppressed by evil spirits and raise a girl from the dead. After all this, Jesus simply sends his disciples out to do as they have seen him do.

"Then Jesus went from village to village, teaching. Calling the Twelve to him, he sent them out two by two and gave them authority over impure spirits. These were his instructions: "Take nothing for the journey except a staff—no bread, no bag, no money in your belts. Wear sandals but not an extra shirt. Whenever you enter a house, stay there until you leave that town. And if any place will not welcome you or listen to you, leave that place and shake the dust off your feet as a testimony against them." They went out and preached that people should repent. They drove out many demons and anointed many sick people with oil and healed them." (Mark 6:6–13)

There are two similar stories in the Gospel of Matthew: the feeding of the five thousand (Matthew 14:13–21) and the feeding of the four thousand (Matthew 15:29–39). In both stories, there's a crowd, they're hungry, and Jesus and the disciples do not have enough food to feed them. Jesus gives thanks for what he has and commands the disciples to give out what food they have. As they do, a miracle takes place: the food doesn't run out. In fact, there are leftovers!

Later, in Matthew 16, Jesus refers to these two events to make a point about the consequences of embracing the teachings of the religious leaders of the day: the Pharisees and Sadducees. Although their teachings clearly had religious form, they lacked the divine power of Jesus's teachings, which are noted to bear great authority.[1]

I love Jesus's approach to training his disciples. "Come watch me. Let's talk about it. Now you go do the same, and after that, we can talk some more about what happened." I know I've benefitted greatly when those further ahead in the faith have taken this approach with me. It's this type of life-on-life discipleship that Jesus models and that can lead us through the grit, grime, and glory of life.

In 2009 I was living on a North London council estate called Grahame Park. I attended Trinity Church, which was located just off the estate. One day I was walking to the local shops, and I passed a flat that had caught my attention. Its windows were smashed, and its garden was filled with junk. I'd passed this flat many times before. It was the home of a local addict.

As I passed, the guy who lived there was standing in the garden, half-naked. He was covered in tattoos and was clearly coming down from a huge binge of drugs and alcohol. I felt a strong sense that I should go and buy the man some cigarettes and a lighter. At first, I was rather unsure about this but concluded it was better to do what I thought God was prompting me to do than to be disobedient. I knew this sense wasn't coming from me. I bought the cigarettes and lighter and headed back to

---

1. In Mark 1:27, we read, "The people were all so amazed that they asked each other, 'What is this? A new teaching—and with authority! He even gives orders to impure spirits and they obey him.'"

his flat. Jesus was going to teach me something that day; I just didn't know then.

Take a Closer Look

We often read that Jesus ministers to people, then withdraws to a quiet place. These little lines in the Bible can easily be passed over. However, the disciples must have begun to realise that Jesus's withdrawal was intentional. They saw something in Jesus that they didn't see in the other religious leaders of the time. In some ways, the situation probably isn't much different from our own. We can also see something in Jesus's life that we can't see in much of Christianity today.

Jesus regularly withdrew to spend time with the Father, showing the disciples he wasn't just another rabbi (teacher) who knew the Scriptures, but one who had the power and authority to demonstrate his teachings (right behaviours).

Jesus's way of life flowed from his prayerful connection to the Father. The Gospel of John reveals a few very telling statements to back up this idea. In John 5:19, Jesus says, "Very truly I tell you, the Son can do nothing by himself; he can do only what he sees his Father doing, because whatever the Father does the Son also does." In John 12:49, Jesus says something similar; "For I did not speak on my own, but the Father who sent me commanded me to say all that I have spoken."

The disciples wanted to learn from Jesus, and it seems they considered learning to pray (communicate) to be the most valuable. I say this because there is no record of the disciples asking Jesus how to do miracles or many other things, but it is recorded that the disciples ask him how to pray (Luke 11:1).

Jesus the teacher taught his followers a way of life that included a mixture of beliefs, spiritual practices, and ways of viewing the world. Jesus both taught and demonstrated these ways and trained his disciples to do the same. These produce in us a Jesus-shaped life, evidenced by the Holy Spirit's work in our lives. What does this look like? It's a mixture of fruits (Galatians 5:13–26) and gifts (1 Corinthians 12:4–11). This combination is evidence of an authentic faith in Jesus.

Converts or Disciples?

In his book *The Great Omission*, Dallas Willard explains that the Western church has for the most part failed to make disciples of Jesus and only makes converts.[2] Converts are defined as those who believe in Jesus but do not practice his ways of life. Disciples, meanwhile, are those who believe in Jesus *and* practice his ways of life.

Willard outlines some harrowing facts about the state of church in America. By and large, the church population of the United States does not live in a way that's morally different from the nonchurch population. I would imagine this is the case with most Western church populations.

Jesus the teacher didn't call his early followers simply to believe in him—to become converts. The established practice of the day in Israel was that students who showed incredible ability were given the honour of sitting at a rabbi's feet—that is, learning from their way of life. To be a

---

2. Dallas Willard, The Great Omission, page 7: "The disciple is one who, intent upon becoming Christ-like and so dwelling in his 'faith and practice,' systematically and progressively rearranges his affairs to that end. . . . In contrast, the non-disciple whether inside or outside the church, has something 'more important' to do or undertake than to become like Jesus Christ."

disciple of a rabbi was an amazing privilege. Apostle Paul speaks of being at the feet of the notable Rabbi Gamaliel.[3]

Why has the Church moved away from this idea of discipleship and toward the idea of conversion? This is a complex issue, but in my opinion, two notable historical events are the primary contributors.

First, Christianity developed under the oppression of the Roman Empire. It was not socially advantageous to be a Christian until Emperor Constantine's Milan Edict in AD 313, which initiated the conversion of the Roman Empire to Christianity. From this point on, the stage was set for people to believe in Jesus as the Son of God—but not to practice or even know of his ways of life. We might call this cultural faith.

Cultural faith is not discipleship; it's fitting in with what's popular. Cultural faith is hypocritical by nature, as it's about being seen to have the appropriate beliefs and behaviours, but there is no internal transformation taking place. Jesus didn't hold back on rebuking those with a hypocritical cultural faith: "Woe to you, teachers of the law and Pharisees, you hypocrites! You are like whitewashed tombs, which look beautiful on the outside but on the inside are full of the bones of the dead and everything unclean. In the same way, on the outside you appear to people as righteous but on the inside you are full of hypocrisy and wickedness" (Matthew 23:27–28).

The second historical event was called the Reformation, which began in the early 1500s. Revolting against the Catholic Church, a German monk

---

3. "I am a Jew, born in Tarsus in Cilicia, but brought up in this city, educated at the feet of Gamaliel according to the strict manner of the law of our fathers, being zealous for God as all of you are this day." (Acts 22:3 [ESV])

and others with similar ideas paved the way for what is now called the Protestant Church. A major theme of the Reformation was the biblical concept of being saved by faith alone. As is stated in Ephesians 2:8-9, "For it is by grace you have been saved, through faith—and this is not from yourselves, it is the gift of God—not by works, so that no one can boast."

The problem with this 'faith alone' narrative is that the biblical authors never disconnected faith from godly living—or living a Jesus-shaped life, as I like to call it. It is not that godly living saves us. Godly living shows that our faith is authentic. This is why the next verse says, "For we are God's handiwork, created in Christ Jesus to do good works, which God prepared in advance for us to do" (Ephesians 2:10).

Jesus our teacher calls us to follow his disciplines and practices, which leads to an authentic faith.

Being Led by Jesus

Back to the story of the addict in North London. After listening to that inner voice and getting cigarettes, I knocked on the window. The drunken rocker hobbled to the door. I told him Jesus wanted to show his love and kindness, then I gave him the cigarettes and lighter. He invited me into his flat, which looked like a bomb had hit it. It hadn't been cleaned in a very long time and smelt like rotting fish. I sat on his broken sofa and began one of the most bizarre conversations I've ever had. Speedy, who was called this because of his addiction to speed and because of the tattoo on his forehead, spoke with me about aliens, government powers, various conspiracy theories, and the like. After some time, I told Speedy I'd pick him up later that evening, and Kaz (my wife) and I would have him over for dinner.

By following the Holy Spirit's encouragement, a new adventure began through Speedy, who had connections with other addicts and those caught up in prostitution. From that point on, we'd gather every week with this growing community of beautiful and broken people, along with some friends from church.

There were so many internal battles to go through as we welcomed these people into our lives and homes—from worrying about our possessions being stolen and that we might be feeding an addiction, to the relational challenges that come up when trying to walk alongside people with such chaotic lives. Jesus took us way out of our comfort zones and used this group of people to transform our mindsets. We may have served them in many practical ways, but they served us, too, by revealing our religious hypocrisy.

Over the next year or so, we gathered up to thirty different people from across the Council Estate, many of whom went on to do an Alpha course with us.[4] Some of them became followers of Jesus, and several were even baptised. Others battled deeply with the addictions and the cycles of brokenness in their lives. Together, we supported one another and prayed to Jesus for guidance and grace.

Looking back, this adventure with Jesus makes me think about how often we stop God's work because of our theological beliefs. Could God really tell me to buy someone cigarettes? Isn't smoking a sin? Is that biblical? These are all great questions, and some still remain unanswered.

---

4. Learn more at https://alpha.org

What I do know is God worked powerfully through me in that moment, and it allowed the Gospel to be shared with people who needed it. It enabled my friends and me to share our lives and faith with those in very difficult and grimy situations, and Jesus taught us much during this precious time.

Seeking to live a Jesus-shaped life, I acted in obedience when I sensed that I should buy a stranger some cigarettes, even though it seemed rather odd. Knowing that Jesus our teacher often sat and ate with all types of people encouraged Kaz and me to do the same.

The real Jesus loves to show up in these unexpected places. He wants to train his disciples to love these places and bring transformation to those caught in terrible cycles. Christianity is not about having a 'nice' life; it's about having a Christ-like life. The real Jesus has solutions for the world's grimiest problems. He wants to reveal his glory in those places through disciples like you and me. Living a Christ-like life can be messy and full of mystery, but it's a much better way.

Prayer

Jesus, today I invite you to be my teacher. I desire an authentic, genuine faith, but I've been misguided or disappointed by the form of Christianity I've experienced.

I ask that you guide me to the right path. Jesus, I trust you to teach me. Amen.

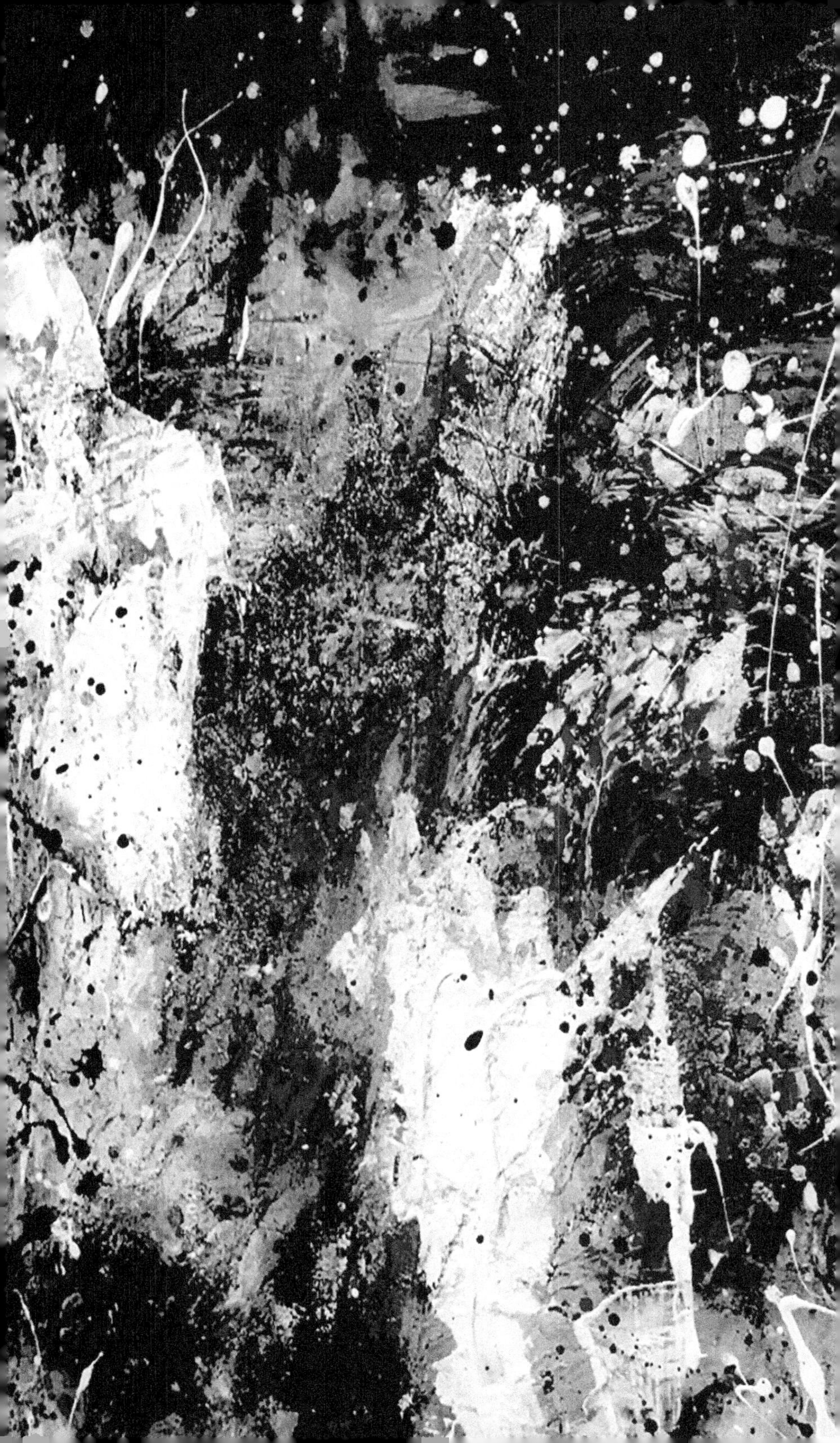

Chapter 4

Where Is the Power?

HAVE YOU EVER BEEN truly hungry or thirsty? Almost to the point of desperation?

For most of us in the West, I imagine this experience is probably very uncommon. But this type of hunger is exactly what Jesus was talking about in the Sermon on the Mount when He said, "Blessed are those who hunger and thirst for righteousness for they will be filled" (Matthew 5:6). Jesus wasn't saying to get off the sofa if you're hungry and get a snack from the kitchen. No, Jesus was saying, "If you're crying out, day and night, for righteousness; for God's rule, reign, and Kingdom to come upon the Earth; for the plague of evil, injustice, war, famine, horror, and tragedy to come to an end; then get ready. That desire is about to be met, and you will be satisfied when My Kingdom comes fully upon the earth!"

Hunger and thirst in this text refer to an unquenchable desire. Jesus is talking about a life-and-death type of thirst and hunger, which His listeners on the mountain knew only too well. For those travelling across ancient Israel, through wastelands and desert roads, running out of food or water would have been a common experience. With no service stations, Starbucks, or McDonald's to stop at during those journeys, Jesus's original listeners knew what true thirst and hunger were and what they'd give to be sated.

There came a point in my relationship with Jesus where I began to desire—in a rather unquenchable way— to see God's power at work in my life and in the church. It's strange to me that someone could read the Gospels and Acts, only to expect a life of following Jesus without seeing God heal bodies, cast out demons, multiply food, encounter angels, and experience supernatural gifts.

That evening after sunset the people brought to Jesus all the sick and demon-possessed. The whole town gathered at the door, and Jesus healed many who had various diseases. He also drove out many demons, but He would not let the demons speak because they knew who He was. (Mark 1:32–34)

Then Peter said, "Silver or gold I do not have, but what I do have I give you. In the name of Jesus Christ of Nazareth, walk." Taking him by the right hand, helped him up, and instantly the man's feet and ankles became strong. He jumped to his feet and began to walk. Then he went with them into the temple courts, walking and jumping, and praising God. When all the people saw him walking and praising God, they recognized him as the same man who used to sit begging at the temple gate called Beautiful, and they were filled with wonder and amazement at what had happened to him. (Acts 3:6–10)

To read the Gospels and Acts and come to the conclusion that a Jesus follower's life should not include any supernatural experiences seems completely at odds with what Jesus, His disciples, and the early church modelled.

Hunger is compelling, and my desire for the supernatural power of God to be more obvious in my life grew and grew. I fed this hunger by reading books, listening to podcasts, and engaging with people who were experiencing what I desired and had lifestyles that included God's supernatural power.

What I wasn't prepared for were the problems and debate such a pursuit would cause. I quickly discovered that when it comes to the church as a whole, there seem to be three groups that exist:

- Those who believe in Jesus but not in miracles.
- Those who believe in Jesus and the possibility of miracles.
- Those who believe in Jesus for miracles.

As I transitioned into believing in Jesus for miracles, I often found myself in conflict with those who didn't believe miracles were possible. Once, at a church leaders' event, I spoke to a man who had gout in his foot and was in a lot of pain. I asked if I could pray for him, and he said yes. I prayed, and Jesus healed him right there on the spot. Instantly, all his pain was gone. I then had a chat with him, during which I discovered he didn't believe in miracles, and I explained why I did. He proceeded to tell me that my understanding of the Bible and God's power was wrong, to which I said something like, "Well, we might need to agree to disagree on this one. But there's no denying that you're now pain-free." It was a strange moment, to say the least, especially considering Jesus had just healed him.

I've had similar experiences many times over the years. It's not a problem I think will go away anytime soon, as there is a great mystery about why God seems to intervene in some cases and not others. Even at this moment, people I care for and pray with are chronically sick, while others are experiencing God's healing touch.

My learning in this area is that those who are truly hungry for God's Kingdom—for His righteousness for His glory—are not easily distracted from their pursuit. They are willing to pay a price to get what they believe is possible. Over the years, I've been questioned and challenged, had those I respect be disrespected and called heretics, and been disrespected and called a heretic myself. Yet true hunger pushes past all that stuff. True hunger is revealed in the grit and determination to find the treasure of God's Kingdom. If we give up at the slightest negative criticism or pushback, we're not as hungry as we think we are. If we are truly hungry for God's power in our lives, hardships and rejection won't hinder or stop our pursuit.

Hunger for God's glory and His Kingdom is an essential part of our discipleship to Jesus. In the Sermon on the Mount, Jesus says the hungry will be satisfied. In our discipleship journey with Jesus, we should be honest with ourselves and see how hungry we really are. We need to have some grit about us.

Risk

If hunger drives us towards God's power and glory, then taking risks is how we discover what God will do through us. We can often understand risk based on a safety model. For example, rock climbing without safety ropes and a harness is riskier than doing it with them. If we were to invest money in stocks or shares, we would be risking the safety of our assets based on the market at that time. We all take risks of some kind.

Risk, then, is about recognising that something is beyond our control and deciding how comfortable we are with that lack of control. Faith, when put into practice, is where we as disciples of Jesus choose to take a risk based on our faith in God. As we discovered in the previous chapter, authentic faith is not just about beliefs. It's about living a Christ-like lifestyle.

My friend from India, Mani, is one of the biggest risk-takers I know. I've worked alongside local church pastors in India for a number of years, and Mani is one of them. We have travelled together through the slums of North India, where infectious, transferable disease spreads like wildfire. Pastor Mani had no issue laying his hands in prayer on any person we came across, regardless of their condition. There was a real risk to his own personal health in doing this, but he was convinced God's power would protect him and heal those he prayed for. Pastor Mani was willing to pay a price because his hunger for God's Kingdom was greater than his desire to protect himself.

One day, we travelled to a leprosy colony. All the men, women, and children suffering from leprosy were a grim sight to behold. It's something I'm unlikely to forget. Although this condition is treatable with medication, it's also transferable. As a team, we'd agreed that there was no expectation for people to have physical contact with those from the leprosy colony. Each person was free to decide how they wanted to conduct themselves.

In the car, I prayed to Jesus about this. I didn't want to try to be a hero and just lay hands on everyone because of my faith. Nor did I want to be so bound by fear that I didn't do what Jesus did in the Gospels, which was heal lepers (Mark 1:40–42).

As we approached the colony, I still hadn't decided how I might respond to what I was about to see. As we met with the people in the colony, hearing how they'd been excluded from society, had little or no physical contact with family and friends for years, and been made outsiders and unwanted humans living separated lives, my heart was torn open and filled with compassion. Courage is a beautiful gift, and Mani's willingness to love these people and pray for them regardless of their condition gave me the courage to do the same. This mixture of compassion and courage enabled me to take a risk and entrust God's hands with my own well-being. God was using Mani as a disciple to lead me towards a more Christ-like life.

Taking a risk is often how we practise faith in the Kingdom of God, though it means letting go of control over our lives. I think this is one of the biggest challenges for Western Christians. We are conditioned to want control, and taking risks requires stepping into the unknown. Our worldviews and the opportunities we have mean we're far more comfortable being in control (or supposedly in control) than allowing circumstances to be out of our hands. In nations where there is greater unrest—politically, financially, or perhaps because of natural disasters—it's easier for Christians to surrender control to God. It's a scenario they are more familiar with. If faith is expressed through trust in God, then the person who must pray for their everyday needs and then has them met in some unusual way will develop faith in God's supernatural ability to supply. Similarly, the person who prays to God to help them recover from illness and then experiences supernatural healing will develop a faith that God can and does heal sickness.

When everyday life is beyond our control, we are more open to surrendering to a higher power. For Christians, this means putting greater faith in God than in ourselves. However, when we grow up in environments where we can buy our own food or access medical care, we are at a disadvantage when it comes to practising our faith. There is a real danger of self-sufficiency when we can control almost every part of our lives because of wealth and privilege. In this scenario, God can seem more like an add-on to our lives instead of their foundation.

Faith grows where it is put into practice and exercised most. If we go to the gym and train, we can accomplish more physically. With grit and determination, our bodies can adapt and achieve amazing feats. This same principle applies to faith. We must exercise our faith with real grit to develop it. When both our material needs and basic needs are met, we're more likely to become self-reliant rather than rely on God. Therefore, if we live in more comfortable and self-reliant environments, we should seek adventures with Jesus that are beyond our comfort zone and control. This will help us grow in our faith as if we are going to a spiritual gym and working out. When was the last time you went to a grimy neighbourhood and served the community there? Jesus wants you to put your faith into practice and take some risks.

Revelation

We can all read about God's power flowing through someone as they cast out demons, pray for the sick, or prophesy with great clarity and insight. But unless you've stepped into those moments yourself, you'll never truly understand the spiritual dynamics at play. You won't truly comprehend what it means to partner with God and see His Kingdom come. There are so many revelations of God and Scripture to be found in the 'doing' of the Word.

Moses went to Pharoah eleven times (an initial visit, followed by one for each of the ten plagues) and said, "Let my people go." Each time Moses followed God's directions, he saw God's power in the most extraordinary ways. Psalm 103 says, "He [God] made known His ways to Moses, His deeds to the people of Israel". The people of Israel understood that God had power; they knew God's deeds. Moses knew God's ways, His nature, and His power because he took risks, obeying and following God's lead.

By taking risks, I've learnt that God will give you the words to say if you follow His lead. He really does know the smallest details of our lives. Sometimes when I walk past people on the street, I sense that God might want to speak directly into a person's life. Often, I pick up on one word, such as *decision*. I've learnt to follow this prompt and start up a conversation. I'll then introduce myself and then say something like, "I sense you need to make a decision. Does that resonate with you?" The person often responds positively, and then God will increase my understanding of what the person needs. God often shares obscure personal details that help the person feel loved and known by God. Jesus teaches this concept to His disciples when He says, "The Holy Spirit will give you the words" (Luke 12:12). The revelation comes when I obey these Holy Spirit promptings and take the risk to act on them. We really do miss out if we don't put our beliefs into practice.

I hope the stories in the Bible and this book stir in you a hunger for God's Kingdom and glory. I hope they lead you to take risks and exercise your faith, and that taking those risks will increase your understanding of Jesus' ways. Maybe, someday, your life as a disciple of Jesus will look more like those of the early followers.

Having a hunger for God's power leads to taking risks. Risks of faith lead to experiences that show God's power. These moments create learning opportunities that simply aren't possible to teach unless you're willing to step in and take risks of faith yourself.

Prayer

Jesus, fill me with an increasing hunger for Your glory to be revealed. I pray that I will see your Kingdom in my life and the lives of those around me. Lead me in compassion and help me take risks as I seek to put my faith into practice. Amen.

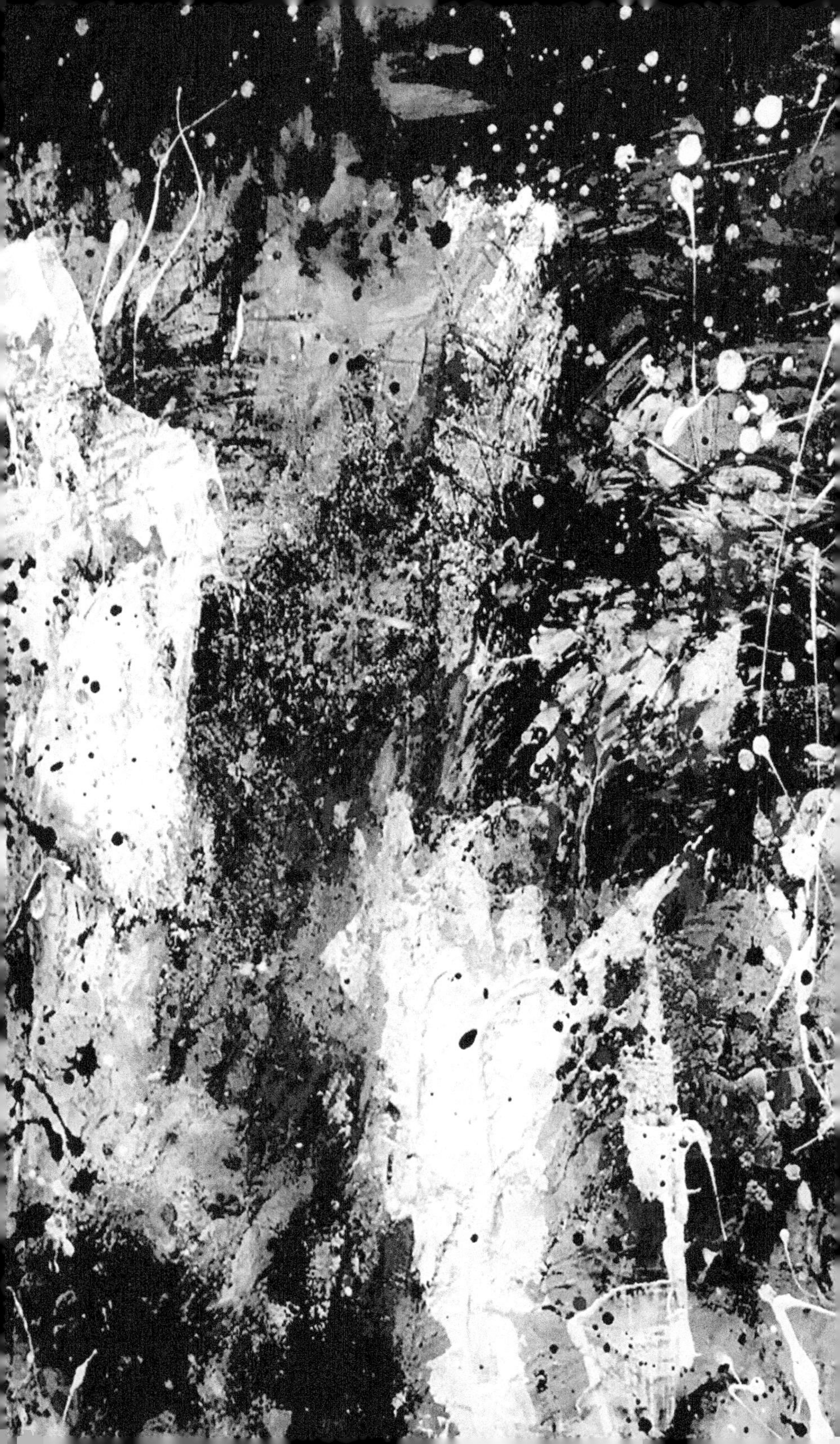

Chapter 5

Did I Hear Right?

I NEVER WANTED TO be a church pastor when I was younger. My dad was a leader in the church, but like most teenagers, I just wanted to be rich and famous and have a big house, fast cars, and regular holidays to some far-off place. Being a pastor isn't exactly a lucrative job, and I was probably a little self-absorbed and selfish. I had very little passion for serving others. But God seemed to have other ideas about what was good for me. He wanted me to live a life not of being self-focused, but of being other-focused—like Jesus, who came to serve, not be served (Matthew 20:28).

When I restarted my faith journey after a time spent rejecting Christianity, I was part of a church that taught serving others was an expression of authentic faith. That helped lay a newer, better foundation in my life. By 2015, I'd been working at the church as an associate pastor for over five years, serving our local community in a variety of ways (not that you need to be a pastor to serve people). I had the opportunity to go to India for two weeks. Like most educated and comparatively wealthy people, I thought I would be going to serve and bless those less fortunate than myself. What I quickly discovered was I was the one who needed a measure of service and to be taught by those who were living very differently from me.

Nations

On the flight queue from Heathrow to Delhi, I met a young man called Gurdeep. He was deeply spiritual and came from a Hindu background but was fascinated by Judaism. We got talking, and when we boarded the plane, I swapped seats with someone so we could sit together. He shared about spiritual things, and I told him what he was looking for was in the book of Ephesians. So from 11:00 p.m. to 1:00 a.m., we spent the early part of the flight reading and discussing the book of Ephesians together. After he'd read God's Word for himself, he became a follower of Jesus. It was at this point I knew something special was going to happen on this trip.

On landing in Delhi, I got on a train to Ludhiana, where I would stay with my hosts. I was exhausted when I arrived at Ludhiana Train Station after almost twenty-four hours of travel. It was around ten at night and very dark outside. As we pulled into the city, I looked out of the window to see small fires and hundreds of sick, disfigured, and disturbed people lining the track in makeshift tents. Grim conditions, to say the least. My eyes were opened to suffering in a way they'd never been before.

We stayed in a brick slum area, where we had to shower with a bucket and the toilet was a hole in the ground. I was assaulted by a variety of insects every day and shared a double bed with a man I barely knew.

Over the next two weeks, I preached and ministered roughly three times a day in varying contexts: under trees, under tarpaulin, in houses, in iron shacks, in nice church buildings, on the streets, and even at an evangelistic rally outside a Hindu temple. The evening meetings lasted for hours, and the queues for prayer were often so long that we wouldn't finish until the small hours of the night.

Life was simple. We slept, ate, preached, prayed, and repeated for two weeks solid.

I learnt to preach without prep or notes, becoming fully reliant on the Holy Spirit. It was terrifying and nerving racking at first. On the first evening, I spent hours preparing a talk only to discover that it was useless in a context where people were illiterate.

The intensity and pace of what we were doing was mind-bending. The colour, the chaos, the ever-present idols of Hinduism—I was out of my depth. Yet I was liberated—free to try things with Jesus I'd never done before. Each night, I'd lay on that bed, exhausted and trying to process all that had taken place.

The sick were healed, evil spirits were cast out, and the lepers were cleansed. In many ways, that two-week trip was the closest I've come to living as Jesus's early followers did. It required a level of endurance and grit and was rather grimy, to say the least, but God's glory was evident in incredible ways too.

It was a privilege to simply get up and share the Gospel of Jesus where I was told to eat what was put in front of me. Life had one focus: to reveal Jesus to those who had never heard of him. The people I got to spend time with were some of the bravest and most courageous I've met. Their lives were simple, beautiful, and filled with God's purpose, rather than the distractions of materialism and media that the West offers.

On my return to the UK, I knew this was not a one-time trip. It was the beginning of an adventure. Over the next few years, I worked with more local Indian pastors and their communities, combining our strengths and skills to educate children, provide medical care, and set up multiple micro-enterprises. Together, we've transformed lives. As a teenager, I'd dreamed of a life of comfort. However, Jesus revealed to me the wonder of a life of service and sacrifice, which is even more exhilarating and fulfilling.

Did I Get This Right?

My time in India wasn't all smooth sailing, though. After my initial visit, I continued to build relationships with the two Europeans who'd invited me out there. I sought to support their ministry financially, prayerfully, and with my own administrative gifts. Over the next few years, we developed a UK charity, for which I became the chair of trustees and the director. We established multiple learning centres for the children in the communities we served, a clinic, and several regular medical outreaches. We even supported a regional hospital and had the local council build a road to our clinic. God was moving powerfully.

As the group of trustees expanded, it became clear that I wasn't on the same wavelength as one of them. We both loved Jesus, but we couldn't agree on our philosophy of ministry or the direction of the charity.

As the emotional pressure mounted, I found myself doubting all the decisions that had made the organisation what it was. Had I heard God right on this? Should I have founded this charity? Our board of trustees was split over certain decisions and the future of the charity. Was this a demonic attack on our work? Maybe. Something had to give if there was going to be any hope for the charity to move forward. I wanted to do the right thing, but what was the right thing? Why should I step aside for a few new team members who had only just become involved?

Eventually, I made the painful decision to walk away from the work I'd invested so much into. Did it hurt? Yes! I was heartbroken. But before I left, my church community gave the charity one final gift to ensure that every project that we had established was funded for the next year.

It was hard to walk away from all of those partnerships, especially the pastors and their families whom I got to know so well. Six years of work lost, relationships over, people I'd served and loved caught up in some grimy web of power plays and control. It made me wonder if I'd even heard God correctly in the first place. Or had I run off on my own adventure and built something that God had never asked for?

I felt like I'd been obedient to the Holy Spirit throughout this journey, but the fruit of the situation wasn't what I hoped, dreamed, or prayed for at all.

After eighteen months of no contact with my partners in India, I reached out to the two families I knew best. Over the following weeks, we unravelled a variety of different stories we'd all been told about each other. We made a commitment to rebuild trust and keep an open dialogue between us. With no trustees and no finances, we started our work again in a much smaller and simpler way. No big operations, just a group of people trying to make a difference in some of the world's grimmest places by sharing the good news of Jesus and serving communities' practical needs.

To this day, I'm still not sure if I made the best decisions the first time around, but this time it feels more like a partnership across the nations. It feels like we've become family and mutually support each other.

This whole process of learning to work cross-culturally has been challenging, but I've seen God at work within my own heart, transforming my desires and attitudes. He's trained and discipled me through hardship and complexities, humbling me in big and small ways so I can be more like Jesus, who gave of Himself for the benefit of others.

Serving across cultures can be very challenging. We can make cultural mistakes so easily. I once put my Bible on the floor, and everyone stared at me like I'd done something terrible. Which, to them, I had! Lesson learnt: never put a holy book on the floor or under your feet. We can also find ourselves operating as 'saviours', which we are not. Only Jesus saves. However, the many challenges of cross-cultural service can be avoided if we are willing to be humble and learn from those of different cultures—to serve and be served.

Neighbours

One of the most famous biblical stories about serving one's neighbours is that of the Good Samaritan (Luke 10:25–37). Jesus defines a neighbour as one who cares. If we are to be good neighbours, we need to care for our families, communities, workplaces, social groups, and anyone else we travel through life alongside. When needs arise in these various groups, the good neighbour is the one who seeks to help. Jesus wants us to be good neighbours to others and follow His example.

A lesser-known passage of Scripture about being a good neighbour is found in Matthew 25:31–46:

"When the Son of Man comes in His glory, and all the angels with Him, He will sit on His glorious throne. All the nations will be gathered before Him, and He will separate the people one from another as a shepherd separates the sheep from the goats. He will put the sheep on His right and the goats on His left. "Then the King will say to those on His right, 'Come, you who are blessed by my Father; take your inheritance, the kingdom prepared for you since the creation of the world. For I was hungry and you gave me something to eat, I was thirsty and you gave me something to drink, I was a stranger and you invited me in, I needed clothes and you clothed me, I was sick and you looked after me, I was in prison and you came to visit me.'

"Then the righteous will answer Him, 'Lord, when did we see you hungry and feed you, or thirsty and give you something to drink? When did we see you a stranger and invite you in, or needing clothes and clothe you? When did we see you sick or in prison and go to visit you?'

"The King will reply, 'Truly I tell you, whatever you did for one of the least of these brothers and sisters of mine, you did for me.'

"Then He will say to those on His left, 'Depart from me, you who are cursed, into the eternal fire prepared for the devil and his angels. For I was hungry and you gave me nothing to eat, I was thirsty and you gave me nothing to drink, I was a stranger and you did not invite me in, I needed clothes and you did not clothe me, I was sick and in prison and you did not look after me.'

"They also will answer, 'Lord, when did we see you hungry or thirsty or a stranger or needing clothes or sick or in prison, and did not help you?'
"He will reply, 'Truly I tell you, whatever you did not do for one of the least of these, you did not do for me.'

"Then they will go away to eternal punishment, but the righteous to eternal life."

The verse that really gets me in this passage is, "The King will reply, 'Truly I tell you, whatever you did for one of the least of these brothers and sisters of mine, you did for me.'" When we serve others, we are serving God himself. That puts serving others in a whole different context for me.

I want to be clear: We don't serve God or others to be accepted or loved. We serve God and others because we know we are loved by God. To say it simply: we get to serve, but we don't have to serve.

How can we as disciples serve our neighbours as Jesus tells us to and demonstrated Himself? It should be simple, but somehow we often overcomplicate it. A great question you can ask yourself is what do you have and how can you share that with another? Time, energy, food, talent, money, listening skills, cooking skills, the gift of hospitality? Do you love being creative? Being thoughtful? The list is endless! Jesus demonstrated a lifestyle of service, and in service, we often discover a joy that is fulfilling in a very different way than receiving.

Football Coaching

A simple way I have served my neighbours is by coaching a football team. I love helping these young boys develop their skills. Each week at the end of practice, we sit in a circle and everyone has to say something positive about the person on their left. It is incredibly powerful, teaching kids to encourage each other. Win, draw, or lose, we are a team that encourages each other, and the boys are happier for it. In a small way, this is also a service to the boys and the parents. After months of doing this, one of the parents commented on the culture of encouragement I had created.

He's from a Muslim background, and I know at some point, my service to the boys will give me an opportunity to share my belief in Jesus with him.

Lunch

One of my friends started a new trend in his workplace. Each day, he secretly made lunch for one person in his office, then placed it on their desk. He did this for weeks as a way to serve his colleagues. After several weeks, someone else started doing the same thing, and now there were two secret lunch-givers. This generous and fun way of serving and blessing someone at work had a number of effects. First, it impacted the culture of the company, increasing its generosity and kindness. Second, it created a sense of anticipation and fun; everyone wanted to know who the secret lunch-maker was and who'd get a free lunch that day.

I'll Smash Your Face In

Sometimes, serving our neighbours can be incredibly difficult. Once, a neighbour and I had such a disagreement about our cars and how they were parked on our busy road that he threatened to smash my face in. Up until this point, we talked and got on well. He'd been over to our place for a few BBQ and even paint our bathroom ceiling. Then, one day, after a shopping trip, his car and my car were parked bumper to bumper. He was furious, drunk and came knocking on my door, ready for a fight. The next morning, I went over to speak with him, but we still couldn't reconcile the matter.

Over the next few months, the atmosphere around our property changed. He and our other neighbour used to sit out in the front garden on a regular basis. After the confrontation, I'd get back from work and just sense his anger with me. I continued to say hello and be polite, privately praying for him all the while.

Eventually, after several months of hostility, we reconciled. Situations like this can be one of the ways Jesus teaches and disciples you. It's like the spiritual gym I mentioned in the previous chapter. In this scenario, I'd gone from trying to love and serve a neighbour to having to love and pray for an enemy. This guy wanted to do me some serious harm, and considering he was ex-army, I'm sure he could have. Praying for him and choosing to be polite required real personal grit. Part of me just wanted to ignore him, and another wanted to retaliate for the threats he'd levelled at me. Over time, Jesus worked on my internal thoughts and helped me wish the best for this neighbour who wanted worse for me.

Each of us has the ability to serve our neighbours with our gifts, talents, and resources. Recognising what we have enables us to work out how we can serve others. When we serve others, we are showing people the Kingdom of God and giving them an opportunity to see Jesus more clearly through us. We also get to be super creative because serving is fun—it's part of God's nature. In service of others God will often teach us many things about ourselves.

Continuing Gifts

The communities I partner with in India consistently inspire me with their courageous faith. Now I regularly get to be on Zoom calls with people who have given up their land, homes, and jobs and have been attacked for their belief in Jesus. It is a humbling privilege. The communities I've befriended might not know the Scriptures or theology like many Western Christians do, but their faith is bold, brave, and beautiful. These people are full of grit, working in grim conditions yet revealing the glory of God. We have much to learn from our brothers and sisters in faith.

We might not all have the opportunity to travel abroad, but we all have the opportunity to learn from other cultures and through serving others. I believe Jesus has hidden treasure in those of all races and ethnicities. As disciples of Jesus, we should be the most welcoming of other cultures because we believe that every person is made in the image of God and therefore has inherent value and worth. Jesus himself was a refugee. Unfortunately, this acceptance isn't always present in Christian communities, but it is God's desire. Revelation 7:9 says, "After this I looked, and there before me was a great multitude that no one could count, from every nation, tribe, people and language, standing before the throne and before the Lamb. They were wearing white robes and were holding palm branches in their hands. And they cried out in a loud voice: 'Salvation belongs to our God, who sits on the throne, and to the Lamb.'"

A church should be a celebration of who God is. Everyone is invited. My friends in India are always teaching me that what really matters in life is not wealth, influence, or possessions, but devotion to Jesus at any cost. They are the most resilient people I know—and the most joyful, despite the hardship and persecution they face. I've long kissed goodbye to those selfish teenage dreams of wealth and fame and found an abundant, joy-filled life doing things Jesus's way: serving others.

Prayer

Jesus, open my eyes to opportunities to serve others around me, both near and far.

Thank you for the gifts, talents, and resources you've given me. Fill me with compassion as you did the Good Samaritan and guide me into a life of service that I may know the truth of your words that say it is better to give than receive. Amen.

For more resources visit
www.jesusmovement.live/resources

PART 2 - GRIME:

JESUS MOVEMENT PUBLISHING

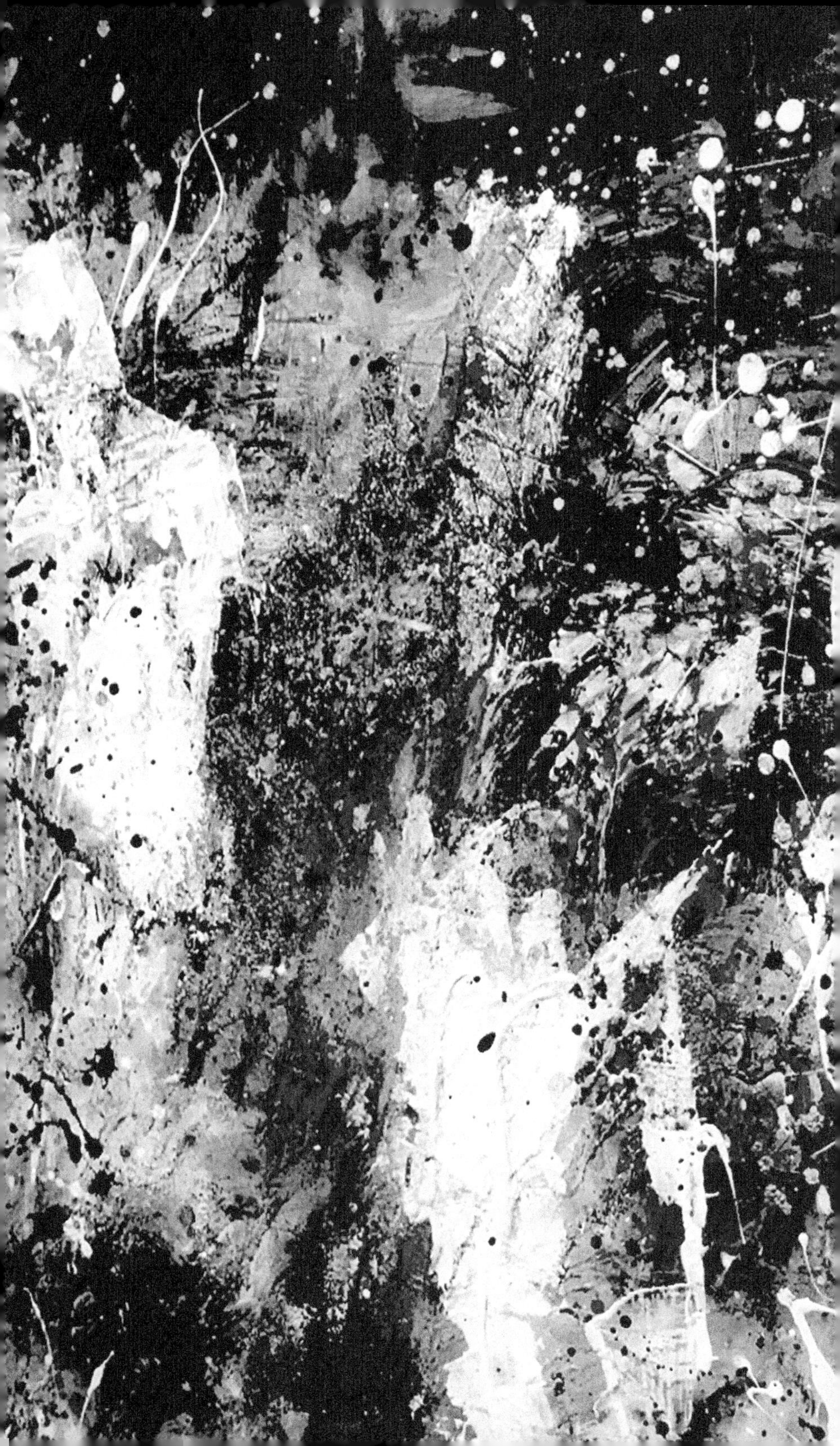

CHAPTER 6

WHY, GOD?

AS MUCH AS YOU and I may wish our lives progressed in a straight line and that putting more time and energy into our passions will yield better results, it just doesn't work that way. Life seems more like a mountainous hike with real highs and real lows. Pain, joy, disappointment, betrayal, love, heartache, laughter, sickness, pressure, stress, glory—they all have a unique way of crashing upon the beach of our lives, destroying or reforming, and not always for our comfort or pleasure. Sometimes the breakthroughs we want cause more problems than they solve. Sometimes the pain is unbearable. Life is full of grit, grime, and glory.

Punishment or Training?

My parents are awesome but not perfect. They love God and have sought to live Jesus-shaped lives. Did they get some things wrong? For sure. Who other than Jesus is perfect anyway? In my early days of learning to be a disciple, I started my own business. In my head, I was going to be a successful personal trainer, earning a £100K salary. I was still working out the wealth thing. In reality, I had mediocre success for ten years, which caused some financial hardship for us as a family. One day, sometime within the first few years of establishing this business, my sister was listening to me moan and complain about God not being there for me. I perceived my lack of profit as God's punishment for the sinful life I'd led, especially throughout my teenage years.

Where had I learnt that God punished people? My dad and my mum? Our UK legal system? School? Church? Wherever it had come from, I believed in a moral right and wrong. When I behaved wrongly, I expected to be punished and had projected this idea onto God.

I believe my dad and mum, just like other authority figures in my life, did their best to teach me right and wrong. As the author of the book of Hebrews writes, our earthly fathers discipline us, and we respect them for it. However, God's discipline and training is perfect and has divine purpose:

Endure hardship as discipline; God is treating you as His children. For what children are not disciplined by their father? If you are not disciplined—and everyone undergoes discipline—then you are not legitimate, not true sons and daughters at all. Moreover, we have all had human fathers who disciplined us and we respected them for it. How much more should we submit to the Father of spirits and live! *They disciplined us for a little while as they thought best; but God disciplines us for our good, in order that we may share in his holiness.* No discipline seems pleasant at the time, but painful. Later on, however, it produces a harvest of righteousness and peace for those who have been trained by it. (Hebrews 12:7–11 [NIV], emphasis added).

As disciples of Jesus, we'd do well to understand the difference between punishment and discipline. This text calls enduring difficult circumstances a discipline. It does not say that difficult circumstances are a punishment from God for the sins we've committed. The word *discipline* is best understood as training, not punishment.

The words *punishment* and *discipline* are almost interchangeable in the English language. But there is an important distinction to be made:

- Discipline is training to reach your potential.

- Punishment is the infliction of penalty as retribution for an offence.

Somehow, I'd come to believe God was punishing me through my circumstances, but that wasn't true. The truth was God allowed circumstances both good and bad into my life to facilitate training. Why would God do that? Well, God trains us so that we might share in His holiness (verse 10). God's training isn't always easy or pleasant, but it is purposeful. It is so that we might share in His holiness and produce a harvest of righteousness in our lives. Righteousness can mean 'right living'. God's discipline, then, equips us to live correctly.

In my late teens and early twenties, one of my goals was to be rich and financially independent, which I'm sure is the aim for many people. I prayed for clients, I prayed for opportunities, I prayed for food when we had none, I prayed for bills to be paid, I prayed for new cars, I prayed for the ability to buy a flat and then years later to buy a house. I cried, complained, moaned, fasted, trusted when it made no sense, and believed when it seemed impossible. Through this experience, little by little, over many years, I've learnt to trust that God is my provider, not my paycheque. He is able to make things happen that are not humanly possible.

Over the years of owning my business, there have been plenty of financial ups and downs, but I've learnt that God is faithful and provides. I am growing to trust in God's provision, and this enables me to give generously, sacrificially, and regularly. Thus, I can live righteously and have peace.

I wonder how God is at work through your circumstances. Is God using a challenging relationship to develop your character? Or is He at work through your finances or health, which cause you to reach out to Him in prayer and develop your faith? You can be sure of one thing: through ups and downs, grit and grime, God is training you to share in His holiness and live rightly.

Pain—or, as the writer of Hebrews calls it, hardship—is often where training takes place. As a personal trainer, I know firsthand that we must push our bodies to the limit, often painfully, to get them to adapt. In the same way, we must also endure times of hardship to grow spiritually and emotionally. They may not be pleasant, but God promises they have a purpose:

Endure hardship as discipline; God is treating you as His children. For what children are not disciplined by their father? If you are not disciplined—and everyone undergoes discipline—then you are not legitimate, not true sons and daughters at all. Moreover, we have all had human fathers who disciplined us and we respected them for it. How much more should we submit to the Father of spirits and live! *They disciplined us for a little while as they thought best; but God disciplines us for our good, in order that we may share in His holiness.* [1] No discipline seems pleasant at the time, but painful. Later on, however, it produces a harvest of righteousness and peace for those who have been trained by it. (Hebrews 12:7–11 [NIV], emphasis added)

Whatever you're going through right now, trust that a time will come when you'll see how it has caused you to grow in godliness. I know it's hard to believe at the moment, especially if something terrible has happened, but there is always hope in the Kingdom of God. True faith is hope in what we cannot see and belief when we don't understand.

Why, God?

We can experience God's goodness and training in those times of emotional pain too.

My wife, Kaz, is an incredible woman of God: passionate, creative, full of life and wisdom. After three years of marriage, she became pregnant. Unfortunately, she had a miscarriage at eleven weeks. This was a painful, challenging time for both of us in different ways. I can't speak for Kaz, but I found myself asking God, "Why?" I just didn't understand why this had happened to us. If God is good and we are following His ways, why would we have to go through such a horrible experience?

I hadn't worked out my 'God is training us, not punishing us' theology yet, so it was easy for me to make some unhealthy connections between my past sins and the situation. Here I was with a heartbroken wife, unsure how to process what had happened while being convinced this was my fault.

Rather unhelpfully, a member of my church tried to comfort me by saying God works all things out for the good of those who love Him (see Romans 8:28–30). True as it may be, this was not helpful at the time. I was racked with guilt, shame, and an overwhelming sense that I'd caused all of Kaz's pain.

Did God answer my question? Not really. Had He been good to Kaz and me? Yes, certainly! When pain and loss crashes in on our lives, our response is often, "Why me? Why, God?" Over the years of journeying with Jesus, I've learnt the *why* is less important. What really matters is who you process your pain with. It is vital we process our pain with God and healthy people. If pain goes unchecked, it wreaks havoc on our lives. If processed with worldly wisdom, it often leads to false comforts such as drinking, excessive eating, shopping, or some other vice. If not processed emotionally, it leads to shutting down emotionally from people and God, which leads to a crisis of faith and damaged relationships with people. Yet if processed with God, Romans 8:28–30 somehow becomes true, just not instantly.

Pain and disappointment are real, and life gets grimy sometimes. As disciples of Jesus, we have to cultivate trust in God's goodness, even when life is hard and we don't understand why. That childlike faith is also where glory is revealed.

During this painful time, I would often listen to a worship album by Brain and Jenn Johnson called *Love Came Down*. I played it over and over, unable to sing along but allowing the words to penetrate deep into my hurting soul. One particular song called "I Will Stay" became my go-to song. Its lyrics moved my soul and gave comfort in my time of need:

I will stay here with You

And watch the world go by

In this moment with You

For the rest of time

All my life here with You

Means more to You than anything

Wasting time spent on You

Is everything

I will wait until we pass through

The door that leads me home

I will stay by You forever

Your love has made us one

Passing time with You Jesus

I will spend my life on You, on You

Pouring out my love for You Jesus

I will give it all just to be with you

I will wait until we pass through

The door that leads me home

I will stay by You forever

Your love has made us one

This song talks about staying with Jesus. The psalmist writes, "Be still and know that I am God" (Psalm 46:10). Both this song and this verse focus on who you are with rather than why something happened. By choosing to stay with Jesus rather than turning to alcohol or some other momentary comfort to numb the pain, we allowed a process of healing to begin. We mourned the passing of this child, knowing we'd see them in Heaven one day. We cried, we talked, we hugged, and we worshipped—often without singing. We played music in our home constantly—sometimes we even fell asleep to it. Music can keep darker thoughts from one's mind. Even now, I sometimes play this song on the piano, and I can rarely sing it without tearing up.

During this time, God really began to unravel my understanding of discipline and punishment. Father God not only healed my heart from this painful loss but also transformed a deep-rooted belief system. The idea that God was more like a court judge handing out punishments for misdeeds and blessings for good behaviour became the image of a loving, compassionate Father who also judges righteously.

Instead of asking, "Why, God?" I've learnt to ask, "Where are you, God?" Who you are within these moments is what really matters. In moments of extraordinary pain and vulnerability, we can easily get caught up in unhelpful behaviours and relationships that give us false comfort and can lead to even worse situations.

If we can change the *why* to a *where* and position ourselves to be with God in the pain, He will comfort us in our brokenness and bring transformation to unhealthy belief systems.

Prayer

Jesus, I turn to You. I've often asked, "Why did this happen?" But today I'm simply asking to know where You are as I walk through this dark valley in my life. Your love has made us one. Draw close to me and lead me through this painful trial. I need to know You are with me, and I choose to trust in Your ways even when I don't understand. Amen.

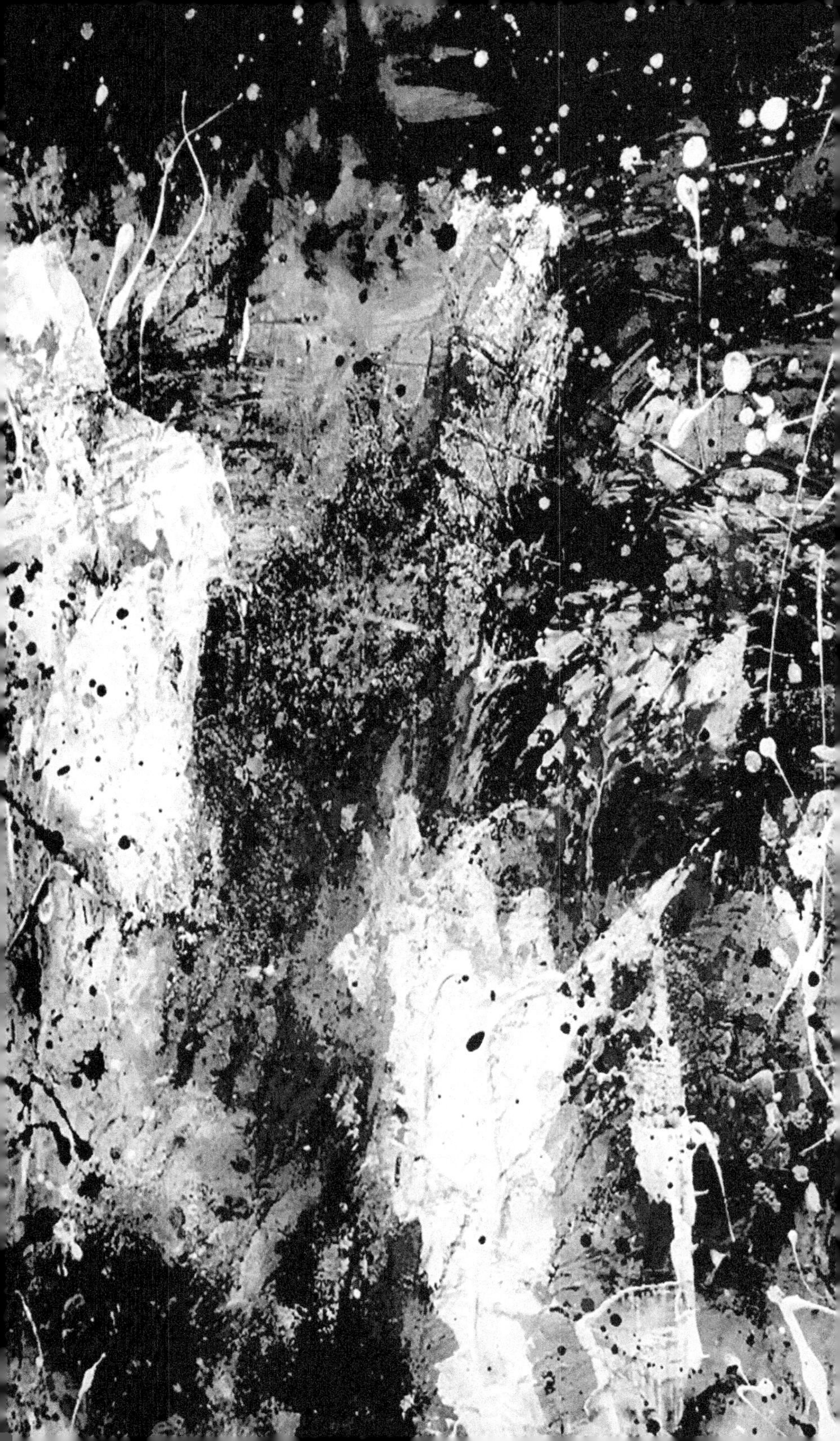

Chapter 7

Hitting the Wall

In October 2021, I hit the wall. Spiritually and emotionally, I was fried. Kaz asked me what I wanted for dinner one day, and I couldn't decide. I don't mean I was indecisive; I was actually unable to make any decision at all. I found myself walking to the chapel and randomly crying in the middle of my workday. Tears flowed from my eyes for no reason, my mental clarity was gone, and the basic decisions of life threw me into a panic. I thought I was losing my mind and grip on reality. We'd just launched our second year of a ministry school, and I was struggling to string sentences together, let alone teach and preach. We were also just about to host a prophetic conference, and I couldn't plan a sermon or hear God's voice at all. This was so out of character for me and incredibly scary.

The church had gone through multiple changes during the COVID-19 pandemic, and we were hosting three smaller in-person services in compliance with the various restrictions and out of respect for people's concerns. We were broadcasting the evening service on YouTube. For two years, I'd tried my best to serve my community and the church, but I felt like I'd failed both. My life, work, and family balance was a mess. During the first national lockdown, I was homeschooling in the morning, while Kaz was at work and then Kaz was homeschooling in the afternoon, and I then worked until late into the night. That might have been okay for a few months, but months turned into years, with all kinds of changes to what we were allowed to do as a church. The pandemic years were riddled with challenges for everyone. As a nation, the recovery is only just beginning, and now we have a major cost of living crisis too.

I didn't know it at the time, but I was crashing. I was hitting the wall. I was about to walk through the valley of the shadow of death. By this time in my life, I'd been following Jesus for fifteen years and pastoring at some level for at least ten. Like most Sundays, I was getting ready for church. I had three sermons to preach over the course of the day. My mind was fractured, and my self-confidence and ability to process rationally or emotionally were greatly diminished. After the second morning service, I told the leadership team we needed to talk after the evening service. When we did, I cried and told them I was falling apart and had no idea what to do.

The next nine months were the toughest of my life so far. I don't really know how Kaz managed to walk through this with me, but she did. Kaz was my rock and my refuge during this time, but also a hidden victim of my breakdown, depression, and fight with anxiety.

How could a church pastor who had shared all these stories and put a variety of spiritual disciplines into practice end up broken, defeated, and questioning the very faith he'd been teaching for so many years? Partly because of the unprecedented effects of the pandemic, partly because we live in a fallen world, partly because I'm a work in progress, but mostly because God isn't looking for people who have their lives put together in some Western ideal of success. God is concerned with our affection for Him and is committed to our training so we might share in His holiness.

This journey through burnout and a mental breakdown was life changing in many ways. I recognise now that my training with Jesus required a season of death, a season of surrender, a season in which God allowed me to experience a breaking point, as Jesus did in the Garden of Gethsemane. I needed God the Father to show His commitment not only to birthing things in my life (being Alpha) but also to ending things in my life (being Omega).

The Father had plans for me, and they were good, but they required the death of my will. They required a degree of brokenness that I didn't yet possess. The Holy Spirit led me through the valley of the shadow of death. I wrestled with incredibly dark thoughts, deconstructed my faith and the structure of the church, and questioned the Western ideas of success that had subtly robbed me.

The book of Hebrews 12:10-11 states that discipline doesn't seem pleasant at the time, but it will produce holiness and righteousness. This challenge took me to the brink of myself yet developed an intimacy with Jesus I'd not yet known. Reflecting back, I now see how this situation enabled God to discipline me which has led to both an increase in holiness and righteousness in my life.

Behind the Curtain

Mental health struggles are at epidemic levels. According to the World Health Organization, around 20 percent of children and adolescents have a mental health condition, and suicide is the second leading cause of death among fifteen-to-nineteen-year-olds. The Bible isn't afraid to talk about the deep emotions we might feel and how to endure and overcome. An incredible Old Testament prophet called Elijah ended up depressed and alone in a cave after an incredible victory against an evil king and queen (1 Kings 19). David wrote many Psalms that expressed an internal struggle. He even wrote about his own soul being downcast (Psalm 43). Jesus has hope for those wrestling with their mental health, but we need to have a honest conversation about it to dispel shame and create pathways to wholeness.

A huge emphasis of this book is to peel off the veneer and show an authentic life of faith—one that's full of grit, grime, and glory. To invite you behind the curtain of my life so you can learn that God is with you through the most challenging and darkest situations. I haven't encountered much talk about mental health and faith over my years of following Jesus. However, the more I've looked into this topic, the more I've discovered that burnout is common in a number of professions, especially those that involve caring for others.

I want to share with you my story of walking through emotional and spiritual burnout. Like a mechanic opening up the hood of a car and taking a look at how everything is working inside, I'll share my private journal entries and seek to unpack how God was at work through the darkest, grimiest period of my life. Some of what I share with you is incredibly raw, perhaps deeply concerning. Remember that I never wrote any of these journal entries to be read by others. They are my internal thoughts, and I've never shared them with anybody before—although that may have been a healthier thing to do. As dark as some of these entries are, I am no longer in that place. God has led me into a much more emotionally and spiritually healthy place.

After some time, I began to rate my levels of happiness to see how I was doing emotionally. Happiness score is rated on a scale of 0 to 10:

- 0 to 3 means I was either wrestling with suicidal thoughts, uncontrollable anxiety, or was depressed to the point that I didn't want to do anything.

- 3 to 4 means I was feeling incredibly low, with no desire to do anything beyond the basics of eating and sleeping.

- 5 means I had basic functionality but no drive and little pleasure.

- 6 to 7 means I had some joy in life and an increased drive to do things while maintaining the basics of life.

- 8 to 9 means I was in a healthy place emotionally and felt motivated to consider goals and work towards them.

- 10 means life was amazing and that anything was possible.

Monday, 11 October 2021 (Happiness Score: N/A)

It's a rather strange feeling to be sitting here writing a journal entry about coming to terms with where I am. Since late June, early July, I've been on a steady spiritual and emotional decline. My ability to make decisions, process information, lead the church, connect with others, enjoy life, hear God, and have vision, a sense of purpose, and self-confidence have all but evaporated from my being. Now I'm experiencing moments of mental paralysis and fearfulness which comes from nowhere.

I feel a profound sense of failure as a husband, father, Jesus follower, and church leader. I have not been able to build or demonstrate the life I feel I'm meant to. Today I'm at home awaiting the doctor to call me. Last night I told the team that I believe I'm having some sort of breakdown, and they said I should take two weeks out. I think a very different adventure is about to begin . . .

I can remember writing this and how true it was. Can you relate to a sense of failure? How has God spoken to you during that time? What did you learn? Let me share some very unfiltered and very honest moments with you during this season of my life.

These first few weeks were head-spinning. It was like I'd been on a roller coaster and suddenly someone had slammed the brakes. Everything just stopped. There was this overwhelming emotional numbness. I felt nothing, desired nothing—like part of me had died. I saw a doctor and spoke to someone at Mind UK. They asked many questions, such as if I was considering self-harm. I wasn't actually thinking or feeling anything, and that was the scary part, but I had experienced enough hardship at this point to know God was with me, and that brought some comfort.

Have you ever felt like this or been close to this level of burnout? If the answer is yes, I encourage you to seek advice from a professional. Don't do this journey alone.

Monday, 15 November 2021 (Happiness Score:1)

Yesterday was a killer after the Remembrance Service, where I noticed my inability to engage with people I know from the community and just felt really disheartened when we went to the church lunch. There was a decent number of people there, maybe fifty. I was totally overwhelmed, not sure who to talk to or what to say. I ended up sitting by myself until a couple of guys from church joined me. They talked about exercise and work, I had nothing to say. I guess I felt empty, worthless, and like a failure. This all sent me into a complete spin. I don't even recognise myself; the person I've become seems so distant from who I was and used to be. I used to be fun, confident, joyful, powerful, and able. I'm so confused. I've been following God the best I can for eighteen years, and right now it feels like I am a complete mess.

Just like Elijah, I was in a cave. Not a physical one, but a very dark, emotional cave. I'd lost my sense of self and purpose. Maybe you picked up this book because you've experienced some real difficulty, perhaps even trauma. Like Elijah, you've gotten to the point where you just don't want to carry on anymore. Maybe you decided to read this book because you need some hope as you battle with your own mental health. Writing a journal enabled me to be honest about how I was feeling. In the next chapter, we look at how journalling can be a useful tool to process your emotions.

Sunday, 21 November 2021(Happiness Score:4)

I feel so far from God, and my desire to worship, read my Bible, or pray just is not there. Do I only have a 'work' relationship with God? Not a 'love, rest, play, and work' relationship with God? Has it always been this way? About doing things for God, not with Him?

Have you ever felt like this? Far from God, with zero hunger for Him? In moments like this, it's good to remember we love God because He first loved us (1 John 4:19). He is the initiator of our relationship, and He is constant in His love for us, while we often blow hot and cold.

Saturday, 18 December 2021

(Happiness Score: 2 going to a 0)

Counselling revealed a lot of pain and the lack-of-trust feeling I have towards God. Mostly, it's centred on disappointment, abandonment, and lack of protection from things way back in my early childhood—ways of thinking that hadn't been brought into alignment with God's Kingdom values. These feelings were overwhelming and sent me into a real spin, where I was so angry and frustrated, I couldn't stay in the house. I felt like a seventeen-year-old boy filled with rage and who had to go and hit some trees in the woods. God, I'm completely broken and an utter mess.

Father I'm totally broken and lost. I cannot live like this, so I've chosen to start taking antidepressants for the sake of my family and mental health. I want to trust You and worship You again. I want to live with You and for You as I once did. Help me, help me, help me. I know you can do all things.

Over the course of November and December, with the help of a professional counsellor, I made a transition from numbness to expressing hurt, pain, disappointment, and frustration. My counsellor taught me this tool called compassion-based therapy, which looks at how different activities are driven by different hormones in the body:

- Red Zone (Adrenaline): Maintains the fight, flight, or freeze responses

- Blue Zone (Dopamine): Motivates one towards achievement

- Green Zone (Oxytocin): Allows for connectedness, bonding, and handling distress

The Green Zone is a place of calm, contentedness, and fun. You typically enter it through what I call 'playful rest'. For me, this would be playing sports, enjoying a beautiful walk or breathtaking landscape, creating a piece of art, enjoying some great food with Kaz, or spending time with friends. For you, it may be something different. Building Green Zone time into your life is vital for long-term emotional health. In the next chapter, I'll outline compassion-based therapy further so you can be equipped to follow Jesus fully without burning out.

As I built these Green Zone activities into my life, I stopped being numb and started to feel again. The only problem was, what I felt was horrible! It was like having a sharp object stuck in your arm and only taking some ibuprofen instead of having it surgically removed. I needed to deal with all the dark, grimy stuff deep in my soul. I needed emotional surgery at a deep level.

Are you open to God performing some major surgery on your heart? Do you trust Him enough to let Him deal with your deepest hurts and setbacks?

Understanding your emotional drivers and your body's natural tendencies is an incredibly useful tool for improving your emotional well-being. Through this process, I came to understand that my default driver was the Blue Zone, and I had to learn how to develop Green Zone activities into my routine. We will look at this more in the next chapter as we discuss more ways to live together in wholeness and authentic faith.

Monday, 31 January 2022 (Happiness Score:3)

Disappointed with church. For a long time I've dreamt of being part of a growing, vibrant church that makes a difference in its community. After three years of building towards this, it feels like the last two years have completely destroyed three years of transformation. Furthermore, leading in these last two years (COVID years) has drained me with further disappointment.

Personally, I thought my own ministry and influence would have increased by now too. But once again this feels like it's diminishing not growing. This, coupled with the fact that I'd hoped Kaz and I would live slightly more comfortable lives than we do, leads me to think:

Dreams + Desire – Reality = Disappointment and Disillusionment

This disappointment and disillusionment make me not want to dream again to protect myself from disappointment. It also makes me question my desires, which I generally thought were God-given. But now I question that too. I think if I was living in some obvious unrepentant sin, then I could accept this perceived difference of blessing and favour. However, I feel I've tried to follow Jesus's way of doing life to the best of my ability for almost two decades. But my reality and my dreams are just so mismatched.

So I ask myself:

Am I really called?

Am I gifted enough?

Why did it end up this way?

Did I subconsciously want parental approval?

Can I accept my reality?

Personally?

With the church?

Are my dreams/desires godly?

Can you relate to these questions? How do you handle setbacks? When I was writing all this out, I sensed God wanted me to read Song of Songs 4. This passage of Scripture describes a bridegroom's desire and love for his bride. As I read these words afresh, I sensed God's love for me despite my brokenness. My prayer for you is that you have more honest conversations with God about what's really going on inside you. As you learn to trust God with your best and your worst, you'll grow to know peace. This is what Jesus began to do in my life as the process of deep heart surgery continued.

In many ways, 18 December was the moment I hit rock bottom and the tide began to turn. January became the first month where I began to express my pain and disappointment.

In my counselling session, we analogised my emotional health to a giant jam jar. In this jar were all my experiences, good and bad. But over the past few years, there had been consistent experiences of loss, disappointment, and pain. The jar had filled up, and I'd simply put the lid on it to keep it all locked up inside. That was why I was so emotionally numb towards the end of 2021. On that day in December, I'd cracked open the lid and, with the help of my counsellor, was learning how to express my pain and disappointment to God and with God. I was beginning to empty this jar of hurt and pain.

Biblically, this would be referred to as lamenting. There are many psalms that express lamentations—a whole book of the Bible even goes by that name. During this time, I was reading an incredibly helpful book called

Dark Clouds, Deep Mercy, which is a superb resource for anyone who wishes to learn how to express deep emotional pain to God in a healthy, biblical way.

There was a long journey ahead, but the dawn was breaking on my dark night. God was equipping me with a new spiritual practice: lamenting. I was expressing pain and finding God in the middle of it. Lamenting has now become one of my core practices, and I'm learning to process my emotions with God. Later in this book, I'll show you how you can do this too.

Sunday, 6 February 2022 (Happiness Score:4)

Recently my sleep has been really bad. I just struggle to get up, and I awake with anxious thoughts about life and a real sense of disconnection from God, Kaz, the church, and purpose. I did counselling today, and it totally sucked out all my energy.

Father, I am really struggling. I am angry, sad, disappointed, frustrated, disengaged, and confused all at the same time. Psalm 18: God delivers and saves.

Thursday, 10 March 2022 (Happiness Score:5)

Father, I know you are good, but I'm struggling to experience it.

Father, I know you are with me, but I'm not feeling it like I used to.

Father, I've really lost my way, my faith, my conviction, but I know you are faithful. Your love is everlasting.

Father, I cannot build this church, but I know you can.

Father, clearly my self-worth and joy are more profoundly connected to my performance than I realise, and I can't perform anymore, so I feel horrid. But I thank you, Father, that you accept and love me just as I am.

FATHER, YOU ARE GOOD. YOU SAVED ME ONCE. DO IT AGAIN.

Thursday, 1 April 2022 (Happiness Score:4)

Father, I recognise that my joy and performance are directly linked, and as a husband and church leader, I feel my performance is poor. I lack the drive, strength, and desire to exercise, serve, care, push boundaries, etc. It is a bit of a downward spiral. As I lack the strength and desire, my performance suffers, which decreases my joy and therefore decreases my strength. But, God, I know your Word says the joy of the Lord is my strength. Restore the joy of your salvation to me and sustain me with your willing Spirit.

Sunday, 8 May 2022 (Happiness Score:6)

Father, I know this is my Garden of Gethsemane season. "Let Your will be done."

Out of the Valley

Your situation is probably different from mine. I'm guessing very few of you are pastors, but many of us have families, jobs, dreams, and desires. This chapter is designed to share the honest, gritty struggles of a follower of Jesus and to start a conversation about mental health and faith that needs to happen. Break the conceit that you must be perfect and have your life together to be a Christian. I hope these pages inspire you to think deeply about your own well-being and be honest with yourself and others about what's really going on and whether you need additional support through counselling, medication, or both. God can handle our brokenness. He is a master potter and can rebuild your life into something more glorious if you let Him.

It's now been well over a year since I fully recovered from burnout and my struggle with depression and anxiety. Counselling, temporary antidepressants, prayer, and lamentation have all been part of my healing journey. I know people will have various opinions on the use of antidepressants, but using them helped stabilise my emotions. They took the edge off the anxiety and the depression. I guess they functioned much like a painkiller. This enabled my counselling sessions to lead me into a new way of thinking and living that I needed.

Over this incredibly grim time, I cried often, moaned, complained, worshipped, read, gave up, hurt people, was prayed for, behaved in ways I regret, read my Bible, refused to engage with God, got mad at God, and expressed myself in very unbiblical ways to God as I learnt to lament.

I've been on a crazy roller-coaster journey. It was horrid, and I have no desire to go back to that place. Am I healed? Probably. Am I changed? Without question. Yet as I look back over this grim experience, I can see God's glory breaking through.

Prayer

Jesus, I desire peace of mind, but I'm often wrestling with anxious thoughts, depression, and sometimes even darker things than that. Walk with me through the valley of the shadow of death. Be my guide and my comfort. Overwhelm me with Your love. I want to follow You wholeheart-

edly, and I know I might be in need of some major heart surgery. Jesus, help me to trust You with all of me both my best and my worst. Amen.

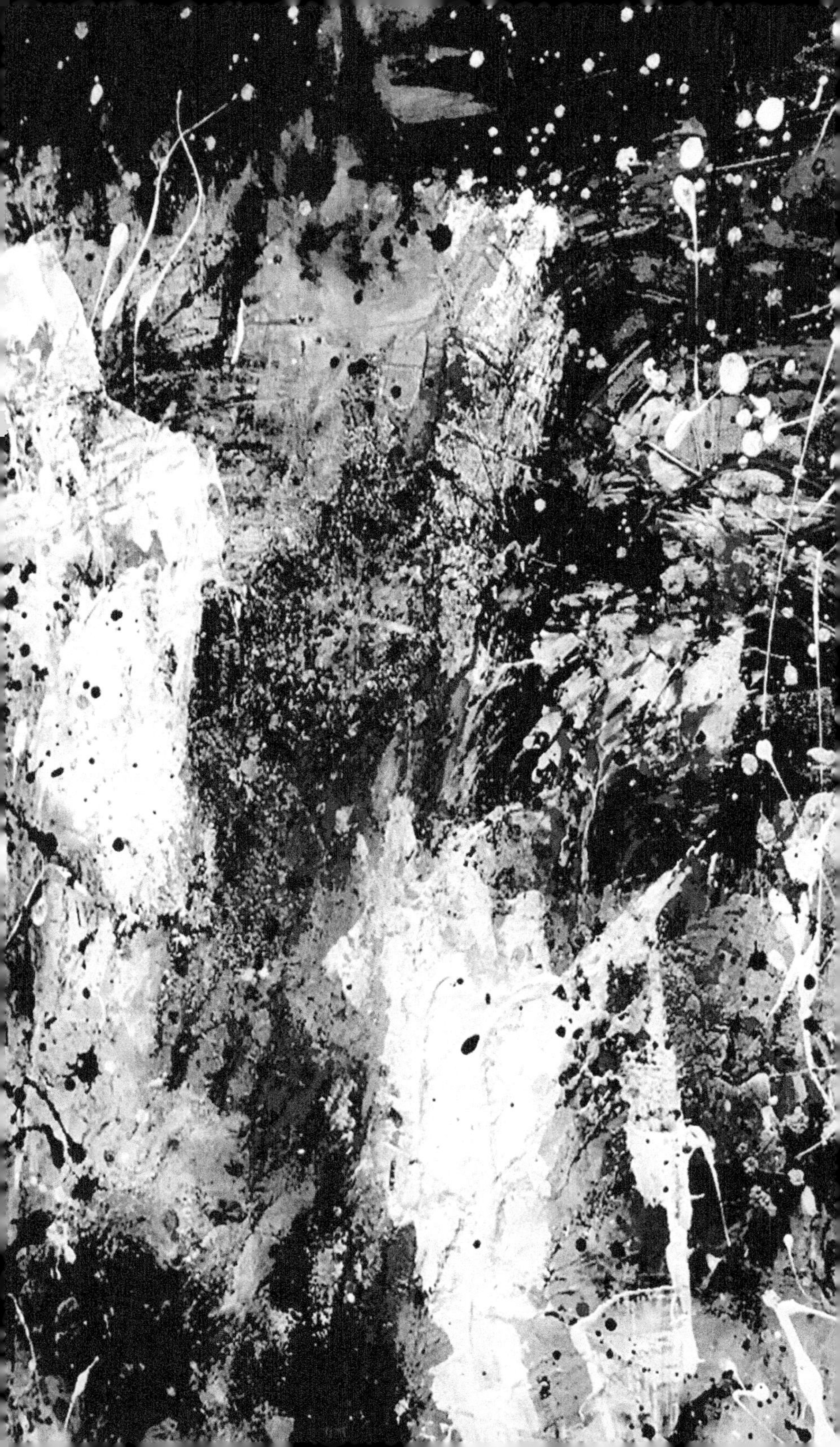

Chapter 8

Tools for Healthy Emotions and Spiritual Well-Being

I don't believe God caused my burnout, but I do believe, in His wisdom, He allowed me to walk through the valley of the shadow of death[1] that I might share in His holiness and produce a harvest of righteousness in my life.[2] This process required grit, it's been grimy, and now His glory is beginning to be revealed.

I've shared the guts of my struggle with burnout, depression, and anxiety so you can have a real-life example of the mess and confusion it causes. Initially, I thought my burnout was like being pushed off a cliff—something that happened to me out of the blue. Now I realise I've probably been living on the edges of burnout since I was about twenty-eight. I had practised a lifestyle without fully understanding my limits emotionally, spiritually, and probably even physically. Instead of embracing those

---

1. "Even though I walk through the darkest valley, I will fear no evil, for you are with me; your rod and your staff, they comfort me." (Psalm 23:4)

2. See Hebrews 12:10.

limitations, I'd tried to override them and do everything. I'd learnt to swallow my emotional pain and fix external problems—or at least try to. I, like so many, would work harder, try to be smarter, learn faster, and so on. Does this sound familiar to you? Never once did it occur to me that I was burying my emotions instead of processing them.

Then that fateful day came in October 2021, and all my emotional junk began to leak out of me. I couldn't override it, so I just switched off emotionally. It was the only option; I had to stop the pain and heartache. It wasn't a logical process; it was an automatic response. I simply shut down because I had no other tools to use at the time.

Do you want to live a healthier, fuller emotional and spiritual life?

The pathway to a healthier emotional life with Jesus was not clear, straightforward, or simple to me. It was a personal journey of discovery and what many Christian writers often refer to as a 'desert experience' that ended up more like Jesus's experience in the Garden of Gethsemane.[3] Jesus Himself came to a place of deep anguish yet said, "Not My will but Your will be done". Jesus chose the Father's will even when He knew it would cost Him His very life. That is true surrender, and one of the mysteries of the Christian faith is that true freedom is found in this kind of submission. I had to keep choosing Jesus's will above my own and surrender more and more of myself. This is a challenging process; we don't like to surrender our possessions, let alone our own will. But this is where true freedom lies. As Jesus teaches, "For whoever wants to save their life will lose it, but whoever loses their life for Me will find it" (Matthew 16:25).

---

3. See Matthew 26:36–46.

I've learnt some helpful emotional tools that I'll share with you. The main spiritual tool I've learnt this season goes back to something I said in chapter 4. God wants us to share in His glory and power, but it will cost us everything, including our sinful human desires. During my burnout, God did his best work on me. Like clay in a potter's hand, He reformed me and transformed my internal emotional life. I passed into a new level of intimacy and friendship with Jesus. I don't mean I've actually earned anything, as that is not a biblical understanding of grace (getting what we don't deserve), but I do believe my relationship with God has developed. God just seems even closer than He did before.

Journaling

Awareness is key to health. If we're aware of what's going on with us physically, emotionally, and spiritually, we can put steps in place to address problems if they arise. However, if we're unaware that a problem exists, we're really in trouble. We understand this principle well on a physical level: if we are tired, we go to bed early; if we have a headache, we take some medication; if we hurt our leg, we tend to the wound. Our awareness of physical pain or stress is more developed and obvious, so we adapt our behaviour to manage it.

Our awareness of emotional or spiritual pain might not present in such an obvious way. This is why journaling can be extremely useful. Taking some time out of our day to sit down, reflect, and write out our thoughts can have a number of benefits. First, the process of journaling can function much like a mechanic looking under the bonnet of a car. As we write our reflections, we grow aware of what's really going on inside us. Second, the process helps to organise our thoughts, bringing order to where there could be an overwhelming sense of chaos.

Journaling regularly allows us to do a quick spot check on our emotional and spiritual health, which can be empowering when we feel overwhelmed and out of our depth.

This is where compassion letter writing and lamenting can be useful tools.

Compassion Letter Writing

The idea of compassion letter writing is to refocus your thoughts and feelings onto being supportive, helpful, and caring towards yourself. Practising this can allow you to access an aspect of yourself that can help tone down your more negative thoughts and feelings. My counsellor, who was awesome and super helpful as I was rebuilding my life after it crashed, taught me this well-known counselling tool. He asked me to write a letter from God to myself. If I couldn't do that, I was supposed to write one from myself to one of my children, imagining they were going through what I was.

A common theme for those wrestling with mental health challenges is that their internal monologue has become highly critical. If we lived in a house where we were constantly criticised, that would be an incredibly draining experience. Well, this is what it feels like almost all the time for those battling mental health issues. Writing a compassion letter helps the person change their critical self-talk into a compassionate, supportive voice—one that is life-giving rather than life-draining.

Here's my first compassion letter. I hope it helps you write your own and experience God's compassion for yourself.

Dear Dave,

I'm so sorry you are going through this. It was never my intention for you to suffer and experience pain, brokenness, and depression. These things all happened because the world is broken, which is why Jesus came to fix the broken and painful experiences of life.

I know you have many questions and feel like you've lost your desire for Me and faith. I'd rather you be real about where you are at than pretend. Being honest shows you desire to connect, which maybe reveals that your faith isn't as diminished as you think. You are just expressing it differently.

I love you and am always here for you. I can handle your worst moments and want an authentic relationship with you, so let's talk about your feelings. No matter how crazy they may seem.

Love, Daddy God

In this letter, I sensed God's love and tenderness, His compassion. Did it fix my problems? No, it didn't. But it helped me experience God's healing compassion and love. The beauty of compassion letter writing is it enables you to experience kindness and comfort. We all have a psychological need to feel safe and protected. When we feel secure, it enables us to bravely explore the world. The way our bodies work confirms this, down to our hormones. As a new baby is cuddled, its brain releases oxytocin, which works to create a bond. As we experience the compassion of others, it creates a bond of trust between us and them, and the same thing happens when we receive God's compassion. God is loving and kind; He is not there to punish you when you make mistakes. No, with compassion and comfort, He restores our hearts and souls.

If you think this might help you, why not write your own letter? Encounter God's compassion, let His love and comfort fill you, and free yourself from that critical inner voice.

Lamentations

What is a lamentation? It's a God-given way of expressing grief, pain, disappointment, or other such emotions. Is that allowed? Well, yes, it's in the Bible. What is its purpose? Lamenting allows us to process our emotions regarding God. We are not simply machines with a logical brain. We are mental, emotional, and spiritual beings, and we need to look after our health in these three areas as well as our physical bodies. A very helpful book on the practice of lamentation is called *Dark Clouds, Deep Mercy* by Mark Vroegop. This book helped me process my pain and disappointment tremendously. Journaling had increased my awareness of what was going on inside me. Writing compassion letters aided my fight against critical self-talk. Lamenting enabled a healthy process of emotional surgery, which brought restoration to my damaged soul.

You can lament anywhere, anytime. Below, I've laid out the basic pattern of lamentation as shown in Psalms, which I have referred to for my own lamentations. This process is very similar to the structure of cognitive behaviour therapy (CBT):

1. *Turn to God.* Basically, direct your pain at Him. He's able to handle it.

2. *Complain.* Fully express all that is going on with you, however you can.

3. *Ask.* Let your requests be made known to God.

4. *Trust.* After doing the first three steps, reaffirm your trust in God.

I practise this process regularly, often without thinking, much like those who have been taught CBT. Lamenting consistently will help keep the heart and spirit pure and free from pain and disappointment, which can desensitise us to the voice of God.

Here is a biblical example of lamenting. I've added our four categories into the text to help you follow this pattern.

Psalm 79: A Psalm of Asaph.

Turn to God

O God,

Complain

the nations have invaded Your inheritance; they have defiled Your holy temple, they have reduced Jerusalem to rubble.

They have left the dead bodies of Your servants as food for the birds of the sky, the flesh of Your own people for the animals of the wild.

They have poured out blood like water all around Jerusalem, and there is no one to bury the dead.

We are objects of contempt to our neighbours, of scorn and derision to those around us.

How long, Lord? Will You be angry forever? How long will Your jealousy burn like fire?

Ask

Pour out Your wrath on the nations that do not acknowledge You, on the kingdoms that do not call on Your name; for they have devoured Jacob and devastated his homeland.

Do not hold against us the sins of past generations; may Your mercy come quickly to meet us, for we are in desperate need.

Help us, God our Saviour, for the glory of your name; deliver us and forgive our sins for Your name's sake.

Why should the nations say, "Where is their God?"

Before our eyes, make known among the nations that You avenge the outpoured blood of Your servants.

May the groans of the prisoners come before You; with Your strong arm preserve those condemned to die.

Pay back into the laps of our neighbours seven times the contempt they have hurled at You, Lord.

Trust

Then we your people, the sheep of your pasture, will praise you forever; from generation to generation we will proclaim your praise.

As you can see from this example, Asaph directs his heart with a cry: "O God". How often do we do that when something goes wrong in our lives? It's almost our first instinct to cry out, "O God!"

What we're not so good at is bringing our full complaint before the One who is able to help us. Asaph doesn't leave much to the imagination in this gritty and grimy lament: "They have left the dead bodies of Your servants as food for the birds of the sky, the flesh of Your own people for the animals of the wild. They have poured out blood like water all around Jerusalem, and there is no one to bury the dead." His complaint is graphic and gutsy. I wonder how often we get this real with God in our communication (prayer) with Him. God is not scared of our complaints. He actually wants us to be this authentic with Him. When we can express this level of pain and confusion, it gives Him the opportunity to comfort us, which builds our connection rather than diminishes it. When we pretend everything is okay and keep our prayers at a surface level, we put a barrier between us and God that should not be there.

After turning and complaining, Asaph then asks God boldly and confidently to be at work in his situation. In verse 8, Asaph says, "Do not hold against us the sins of past generations; may Your mercy come quickly to meet us, for we are in desperate need." His request reveals his faith. Asaph believes God is able to deliver him and the nation from their oppression. It seems crazy to say, but not asking God for things shows we lack faith.

As Asaph moves through this process of lamenting, we see his journey of turning to God, complaining, asking, and finally trusting. The psalm ends with a glorious, confident assertion: "Then we Your people, the sheep of Your pasture, will praise You forever; from generation to generation we will proclaim Your praise."

Writing our own personal lament can be an incredibly helpful tool when navigating the trials of life. Turning, complaining, asking, and trusting is such a simple yet profound biblical practice that can enable you to live an emotionally and spiritually healthy life.

Compassion – Focused Therapy (CFT) Overview

Dr. Raymond Gilbert, a British clinical psychologist, suggests that the human brain can cause an internal critical voice that affects well-being. The human brain has the capacity for caring emotions and positive motives that offset the potential for the destructive thoughts of one's critical voice. Knowing this, Dr. Gilbert created CFT to help people develop the ability to mindfully access and redirect their emotions and motives towards themselves and others, thus cultivating inner compassion that is stronger than destructive behaviours.

So, how does this process work exactly? Research indicates that humans hold at least three different emotion regulation systems: threat and self-protection, drive and excitement, and content and soothing.

- *Threat and Self-Protection (Red Zone).* This system is what generates fear, anger, and disgust to offer mental and physical protection.

- *Drive and Excitement (Blue Zone).* This system is what motivates people to seek out things like food, shelter, and other people to form relationships with.

- *Content and Soothing (Green Zone).* This system is activated when a person is fulfilled by what they have, feels peaceful, and no longer needs to look for outside resources.

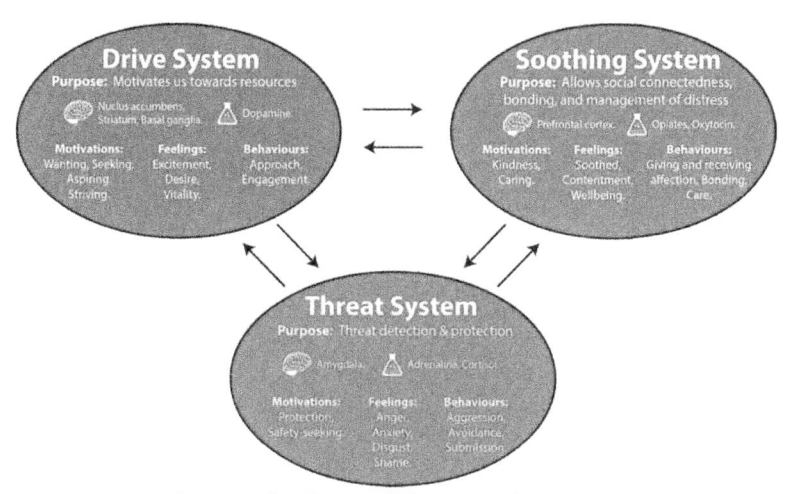

Compassion Focused Therapy Drive System

Mental illnesses such as depression and anxiety can surface as a direct result of an imbalance between these three emotional systems. For example, people who are self-criticising or have chronic feelings of shame likely did not have enough soothing stimulation (Green) and too much stimulation within their threat system (Red). In these cases, feeling compassion for themselves and others can pose a struggle, making them more sensitive to rejection and criticism. This is where CFT comes into play, as these techniques are designed to create a balance between the three systems to increase compassion while simultaneously treating other concurring issues, such as trauma, abuse, or neglect.

As I worked on finding balance, I realised how often I functioned out of the Blue Zone and how infrequently the Green Zone was in my life. I encourage you to take time to reflect on your life and your weekly habits. Jesus didn't just tend to His work/ministry; He rested, enjoyed time with friends, and took time out. Jesus had a Green Zone. He modelled a balanced approach to life, not a hurried, harassed, and busy one. Jesus's burden is easy and light, and He promises us rest (Matthew 11:29–30). Rest is a gift we would do well to accept.

Life is grimy, and we need grace and grit to endure the ups and downs. I hope sharing my story gives you confidence that God can restore you to glory once again. Journaling, writing compassion letters, lamenting, and having a basic understanding of CFT can help you process your emotions in a healthy, biblical way. God's Word promises us that we will go from one degree of glory to another (2 Corinthians 3:17–18), and I can attest to this. It often doesn't feel like it, though. As the author of Hebrews says:

Endure hardship as discipline; God is treating you as His children. For what children are not disciplined by their father? If you are not disciplined—and everyone undergoes discipline—then you are not legitimate, not true sons and daughters at all. Moreover, we have all had human fathers who disciplined us and we respected them for it. How much more should we submit to the Father of spirits and live! They disciplined us for a little while as they thought best; but God disciplines us for our good, in order that we may share in His holiness. *No discipline seems pleasant at the time, but painful. Later on, however, it produces a harvest of righteousness and peace for those who have been trained by it.* (Hebrews 12:7–11 [NIV] emphasis added)

Jesus's best for us is not faith in which we burn out or give up, but one of emotional and spiritual health. A life that is attractive and full of joy (John 10:10).

Prayer

Jesus, I turn to You. My heart's cry is, "O God!" Teach me to trust You with my whole heart, with my deepest pain and complaint. Give me faith to ask for Your deliverance, as Asaph did. Holy Spirit, fill me with peace and confidence and total trust so I can live wholeheartedly for Jesus.

For more resources visit
www.jesusmovement.live/resources

PART 3 – GLORY:

JESUS MOVEMENT PUBLISHING

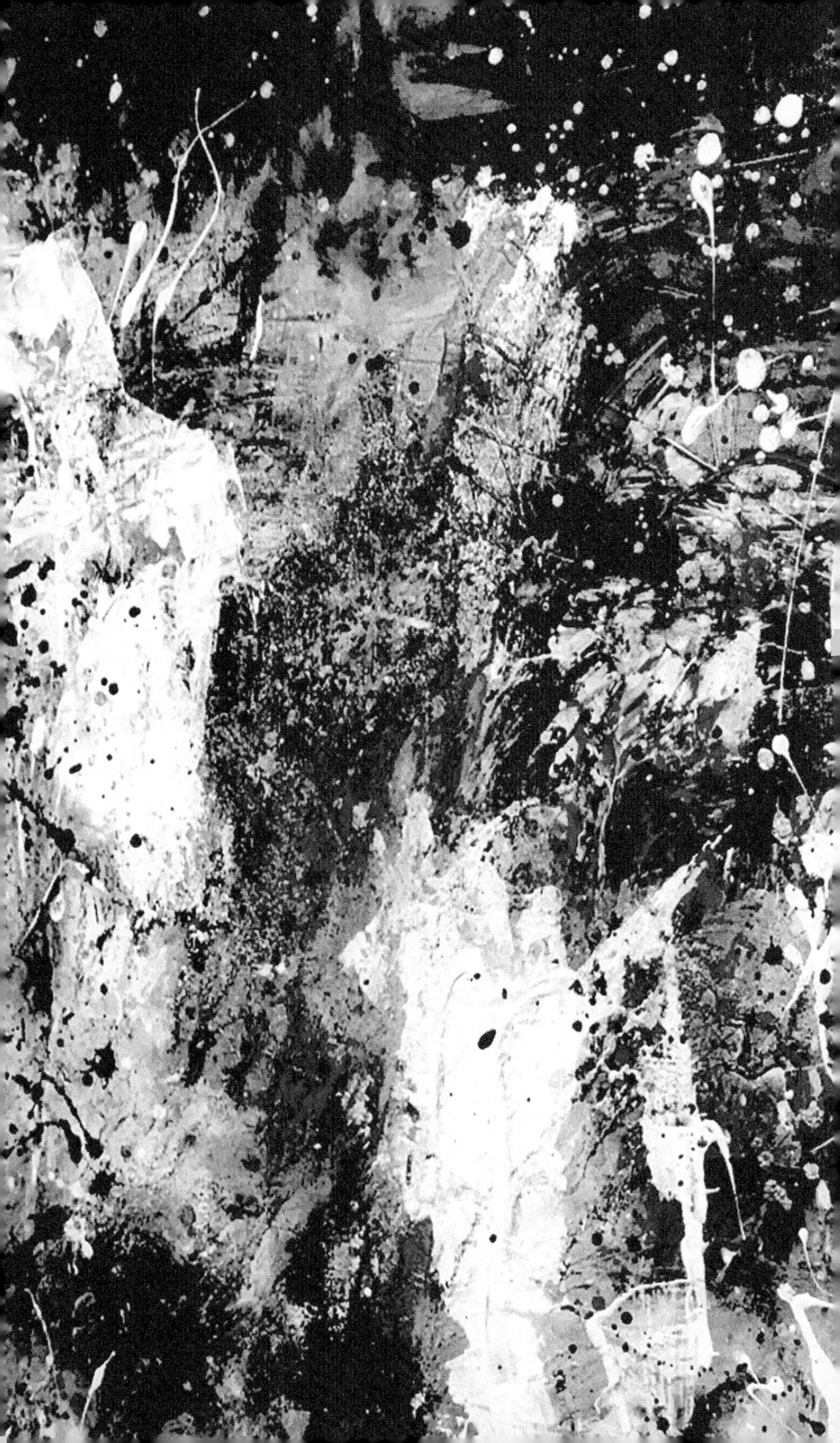

Chapter 9

Mountains and Valleys

TOGETHER, WE HAVE DELVED into some of the grittiest and grimiest experiences of my life and seen how God has been at work in them and through them. I'm sure He is in your life too. As we move towards the end of our journey together, there are a few more key lessons I'd like to share with you about being a disciple of Jesus.

My friend and mentor, Andy Robinson, and I were having a conversation, and he made a throwaway comment about something he calls 'silver-bullet thinking'. Silver-bullet thinking is when church leaders are convinced they've missed the special ingredient that will cause their church to grow. The story goes like this:

- The church leader's church starts growing.

- Other church leaders get interested, wondering why this church is growing and theirs isn't.

- They seek some sort of audience with this church leader to find out what the key to their success (the silver bullet).

- The church leaders talk, and the one with the growing church says, "I'm not sure what we're doing different. God just seems to be moving, and we started doing X."

- The church leader with the stagnating church goes back to their team and says, "We need to start doing X."
- That church starts doing X, but it doesn't get the same result.

Over the years, I've seen this happen countless times—and have even done it myself. It wouldn't surprise me if a very similar phenomenon happens in the business world, especially because we do this in our personal lives. We see others growing in Christ in a way we want to and wonder what the 'silver bullet' is.

After many years of doing this type of thing, I'm convinced we've got it wrong.

The problem with silver-bullet thinking is it mitigates God's unique design for our lives. The wisdom of God is often foolishness to man.[1] We want a one-size-fits-all methodology, but God wants intimate relationships that are unique to every disciple of Jesus.

Matthew 11:16-19 says:

"To what can I compare this generation? They are like children sitting in the marketplaces and calling out to others: [1]"'We played the pipe for you, and you did not dance; we sang a dirge, and you did not mourn.' For John came neither eating nor drinking, and they say, 'He has a demon.' The Son of Man came eating and drinking, and they say, 'Here is a glutton and a drunkard, a friend of tax collectors and sinners.' But wisdom is proved right by her deeds."

---

1. 1 Corinthians 1:18

Wisdom is proven right by her deeds. God moves through people and churches in different ways at different times. One uses a dirge as a message of mourning, the other has a pipe as a message of celebration and hope, yet both are full of the wisdom of God. They are both true at the same time. But in our human reasoning, it can only be one or the other. We are looking for the quick fix, the step-by-step method we can follow. But if God is our shepherd and we are His sheep, it is hearing His voice, following His lead, and maintaining a proximity to Him that are key to our discipleship, not methodology.

The Father has made us uniquely in His image. We are all fearfully and wonderfully made. We each have a unique personality and a blend of perspectives and talents. The apostle Paul encourages us to run our own race (1 Corinthians 9:24). We are not called to run in someone else's race or someone else's lane, just our own, which we are especially created for. How often do we compare ourselves to others and try and get into someone else's lane? When we do this, we miss out on the blessings God has uniquely purposed for us.

In His brilliance, God has called each of us to our own special assignments, each of which fits our wonderfully one-off makeup of gifts, talents, perspectives, resources, times in history, and personality types. That's how amazing our God is.

Build on Your Strengths

Since we are fearfully and wonderfully made, both our strengths and weaknesses can be used for Kingdom purposes. Growing up, I thought being dyslexic was a disadvantage, something I needed to overcome to live fully. Teachers always told me it was a 'problem' that needed to be fixed. The beauty of God's creation is dyslexia; my 'weakness' is part of who I am. I've had additional education to help me manage my dyslexia, but if you ask my family, friends, or church, they will all attest to my terrible spelling, grammar, and reading ability. However, God has used my dyslexia to build His Kingdom because being dyslexic gives me a different set of advantages that non-dyslexics don't have. I can simplify information in an unusual way, and my memory recall seems far more developed than most people I know. I don't think linearly and therefore have excellent problem-solving and entrepreneurial skills. My English skills might be lacking, but I have other God-given strengths.

In Ephesians 4, the apostle Paul talks about Jesus Christ giving gifts to the church. These gifts are people; apostles, prophets, evangelists, pastors, and teachers. They exist to strengthen and build up the Church (the people of God and disciples of Jesus) so they'll be united and mature. I believe each of these people provides a unique perspective:

- The apostle is focused on Heaven's mission.
- The prophet focuses on Heaven's Word, wisdom, and the glory of God.
- The evangelist insists on seeing the lost saved.
- The pastor ensures their church is cared for.
- The teacher focuses on what is true.

As you read that list, I wonder which description most resonated with you. Do you focus on what's true? Are you the type of person who is highly objective? Are you more mission-minded, having some internal sense of an injustice that needs to be changed to bring others freedom? Do you love spiritual things and are fascinated by the more out-of-this-world experiences life can offer? Are you the type of person who says things like, "Why are we in this church building when the lost and unbelieving are outside?" Do you deeply empathise with people's struggles and seek to walk alongside them? In the footnote is a link to a questionnaire which will help you better .[2]

We all carry aspects of these gifts within us, but in my experience, most people tend to favour one or two of them. They are how we see the world. However, this can often minimise others perspectives when they don't fit our own. The evangelist cannot understand why the church meets in a building when the lost are outside. The pastor wants to ensure people are trained before they are sent out on missions, to make sure they are 'safe'. The prophet senses God's presence and often carries a message that no one else understands, so they get frustrated. The teacher wants everything to be true and right, to make sure it's in the Word. The apostle just wants to crack on and do the stuff. The church (the people) is at its best when all these perspectives are involved in the decision-making process, and we are equipped with each of these God-given gifts and perspectives.

However, it's clear why people with different perspectives can find it hard to agree. God desires an equipped and powerful people. Typically, people reach an agreement through compromise. However, regarding these gifts, I suggest compromise is the worst thing we can do. We want the evangelist to be as evangelistic as possible. We want the pastor to really care for people. If each gift were compromised to facilitate harmony in the church, God's people would be ill-equipped. Therefore, it's better to

---

2. https://fivefold.3dmovements.com/

think of these gifts as functioning not through compromise but through tension—sometimes leaning more in one direction and sometimes more in another. Tension produces strength when opposite forces pull against each other. A good example of this is a ballet duo, who use tension to create a pose, lift, or beautiful moves that aren't possible on their own. In a similar way, the five different gifts pull against each other in a healthy dance of tension, not compromising but being fully themselves. Through this tension, God's people can be more thoroughly equipped.

Imagine for a moment that these five types of people are all on a sailboat.

- The apostles would function as the ship's captain, steering the boat successfully while on its sea voyage.

- The prophet would be in the crow's nest, providing the captain with foresight for the journey ahead.

- The evangelist would oversee the recruitment of additional crewmen for the journey.

- The pastor would function as both the ship's cook and its medic, maintaining the health of the crew.

- The teacher would be in charge of the ship's maintenance, ensuring it is always sound to sail.

These five gifts need to work together to have a successful voyage, and that is exactly what Paul is saying in Ephesians 4. All must work together in interdependence upon one another—not in compromise, but as partners in a shared mission.

God's intention is that unity, maturity, and preparedness are brought by those carrying these types of gifts in a greater measure. They in turn share their knowledge and perspectives with the rest of us. We then have the opportunity to grow and learn. We receive from these gifted individuals through humility, which prepares us to become mature disciples of Jesus. Maturity, then, is about being fully developed in each of these perspectives and associated gifts, while unity is about listening well, honouring others' perspectives and gifts, and celebrating our differences. Our model for this is the Trinity (Father, Son, and Holy Spirit). Each member of the Godhead is filled with divine power and wisdom. Each member of the Trinity could rule over the universe on their own, but they function perfectly as One through deference and mutual submission.

As disciples of Jesus, we should not cover our 'weaknesses' by working on them but by functioning in teams. That's one of the reasons I believe Jesus sent his disciples out in twos. Just to be clear, we should of course work towards becoming holy, consistent, God-like characters—the best possible versions of ourselves. However, when it comes to our gifts, if you are not a skilled musician but fantastic at hosting people, don't waste time trying to develop your musical abilities. Be the best host you can be and let others hone their musical skills. If you are a teacher, be a teacher. If you're an apostle, be an apostle. If you're a pastor, be a pastor.

Mountain High, Valley Low, Keep Going

Many events in the Bible occur on mountains and in valleys. Mountains symbolise encounters with God since they are closer to the heavens. Consequently, there are many significant mountaintop moments in the Bible. Moses was given the Ten Commandments on a mountain. Elijah revealed God's power to Israel on Mount Carmel. Jesus gave his most famous sermon on a mountain. Jesus was transfigured on a mountaintop.

The symbolic meaning of a valley is more varied. It can mean a place of transition, fertile land, or a place of spiritual battle. David fought Goliath in the Valley of Elah. Ezekiel called forth a dead army in the valley of dry bones. The Valley of Hinnom outside of Jerusalem was a giant rubbish dump and is often referenced as Gehenna or Hell. It was a horrid place where people sacrificed their children by burning them to death as an act of worship to the false god Molech.

My favourite valley name must be Ono. When said in English, it sounds like *Oh no!* This valley features in the story of Nehemiah. Nehemiah is working with the people of Israel to restore the walls of Jerusalem. Walls signify protection, safety, and dignity. The fact that Jerusalem had no walls was significant. Nehemiah was rebuilding the walls, and Israel's enemies were not happy about it. Nehemiah's opponents called him out to the Valley of Ono. How often does this happen to us? We are doing something of worth for God, and suddenly a problem, a distraction calls us out to a 'valley' away from our work, and we end up saying, "Ono!"

This is such a crucial principle to understand when going to a conference, retreat, class, prayer meeting, or church gathering. These events can be like going to the mountaintop where you receive revelation and encounter God. This is often where we get a vision of something we could do or gain a better understanding of our calling. But when we come down the mountain, from that 'high' experience, and get to work building the thing God has told us about, we often encounter opposition, frustration, and trials. The devil and demonic forces at work in people and circumstances don't want us to have an impact for Jesus. They will resist us, no question. But don't stop building what God has shown you. Do not go into the Valley of Ono to fight your opponents. Just keep building what God has told you to build.

When Paul was defending his ministry to a church who were causing him all kinds of problems, calling him to the Valley of Ono, he handled the situation in a way I love. He said:

And I will keep on doing what I am doing in order to cut the ground from under those who want an opportunity to be considered equal with us in the things they boast about. For such people are false apostles, deceitful workers, masquerading as apostles of Christ. And no wonder, for satan himself masquerades as an angel of light. It is not surprising, then, if his servants also masquerade as servants of righteousness. Their end will be what their actions deserve. (2 Corinthians 11:12–15)

Over the years, I've seen so many disciples of Jesus start working on a great mountaintop idea. Unfortunately, it seems they often lack the consistency and the grit to finish what they started. They stop doing what they were called to do and become distracted, disappointed, or disillusioned. One way or another, they end up in the Valley of Ono rather than building what they were called to build. They are like the seed that fell on the path or that grows up among the thorns:

Listen then to what the parable of the Sower means: When anyone hears the message about the kingdom and does not understand it, the evil one comes and snatches away what was sown in their heart. This is the seed sown along the path. The seed falling on rocky ground refers to someone who hears the word and at once receives it with joy. *But since they have no root, they last only a short time. When trouble or persecution comes because of the word, they quickly fall away. The seed falling among the thorns refers to someone who hears the word, but the worries of this life and the deceitfulness of wealth choke the word, making it unfruitful.* But the seed falling on good soil refers to someone who hears the word and understands it. This is the one who produces a crop, yielding a hundred, sixty or thirty times what was sown. (Matthew 13:18–23 [NIV], emphasis added)

To be truly fruitful as disciples of Jesus in the Kingdom of God, we need to develop the ability to walk obediently and consistently in the same direction for a long time. *Consistency* and *obedience* aren't exactly the most exciting words, are they? We tend to want extraordinary breakthroughs, divine healing, and prophecies—not obedience, long suffering, consistency, or patience. Yet Jesus's ministry expressed both. He was consistently obedient and focused on the task at hand, and miracles, signs, and wonders flowed as He walked to the Father's voice.

May God raise up a generation of disciples who refuse to go to the Valley of Ono. Who refuse distraction, disappointment, or disillusionment. Who are less focused on the instant breakthrough. Who, like Jesus, are willing to walk the long path of obedience.

In our modern world, we love quick fixes. We love instant gratification. However, few people would go to a restaurant expecting a microwave dinner. A convenient meal is never as good as one prepared by a chef. My prayer is that God will grant us disciples who prefer the slow-cooker version of Christianity as opposed to the microwave version we so often see. It's this authentic, gritty, grimy, glorious Christianity that the world is hungry for, and for which we've been looking throughout this book. Let's be those genuine disciples who practise Jesus's way of life in the twenty-first century—not just believing that Jesus is our Saviour, but living like He is our Lord as well.

Prayer

Jesus, in every mountaintop encounter, I pray to know You more. I ask for further revelations of Your nature and Your wonders. Through every valley, help me to endure with grace, to not be disillusioned or distracted, and with consistent obedience to build Your Kingdom and push back darkness. Amen.

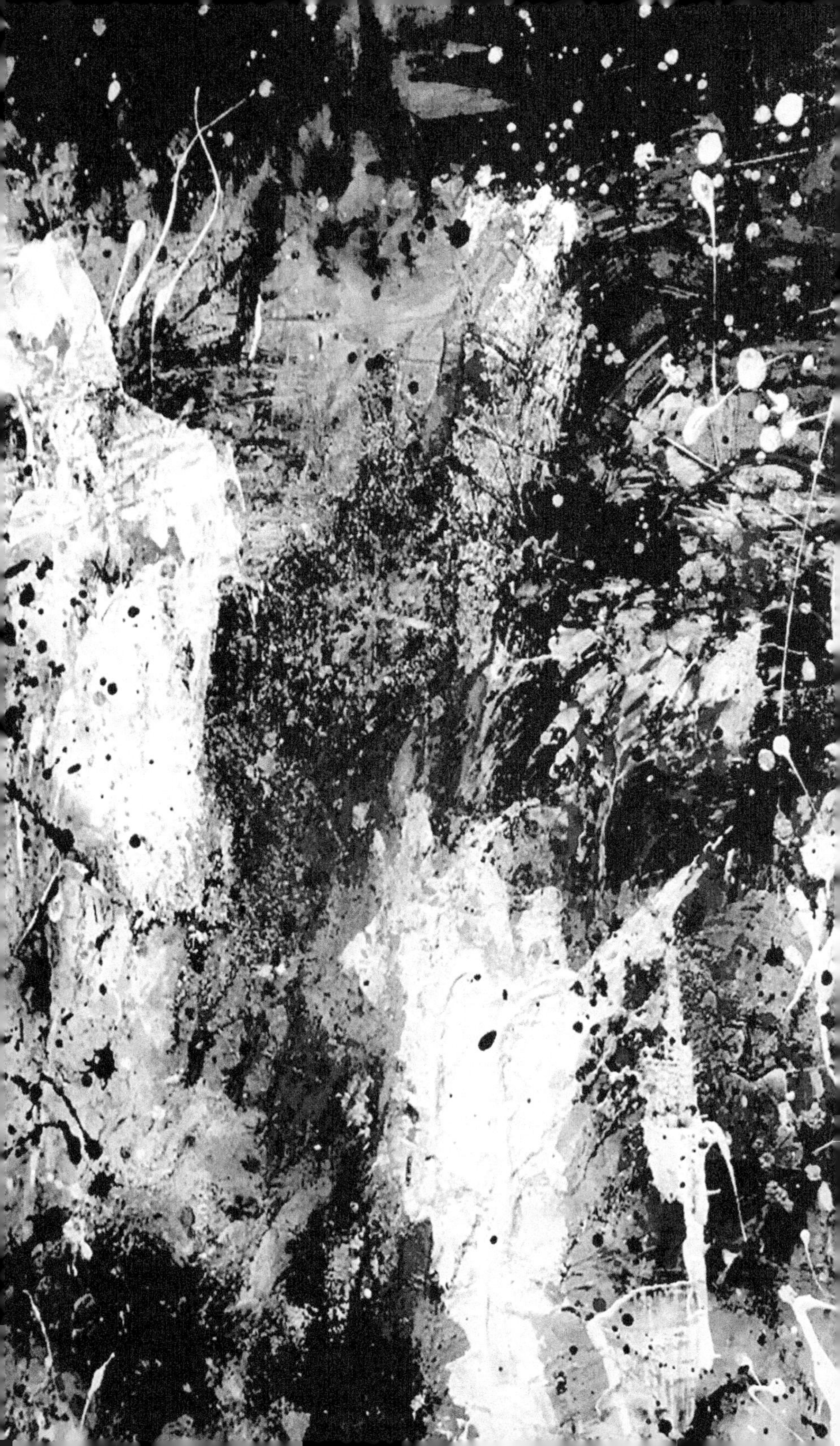

Chapter 10

Making God Known

Growing up in a Christian home and being mocked at school for my parents' faith and the beliefs that they taught me had a profound effect on my life. When I was following the ways of Jesus based on my own personal convictions, I had to learn how to overcome rejection, ridicule, and that uneasy feeling one often gets when talking about Jesus with someone who doesn't yet believe.

Having spoken with many Christians about how confident they feel sharing their faith, I know this is a journey many believers must take. Jesus tells His disciples to "go and make disciples of all nations" (Matthew 28:19). ' teachings with others is part of how we express our faith, yet many Christians really struggle with this—myself included.

We might feel embarrassed, we might not want to cause offence, or we might feel we don't know enough. The list of reasons why it's uncomfortable to share our faith is endless. Over the years, I've learnt some helpful tools for sharing Jesus with others. However, feeling equipped isn't the same as feeling at peace and confident enough to share. There are three areas of learning that have equipped me to overcome that initial trepidation:

1. Sharing Jesus so people move up the Engle scale

2. Listening to understand, not to respond

3. Focusing on honour and love

The Engle Scale

This tool can give us valuable insight into a person's journey with God. Nobody starts in exactly the same place as another, and no one's journey to faith in Jesus is exactly the same. The better we understand where people are on their journey, the easier it is to know how to engage or respond. The Engle Scale of Evangelism can help us categorise where people are on their journey.[1] You may find it helpful to place yourself on this simplified version of the scale, along with a few family members and close friends.

Sharing Jesus, Moving Along the Engle Scale

Sharing Jesus with people only takes a moment, but their journey into a relationship with Jesus often has a long backstory. When I was a personal trainer at a gym in North London, I tried my best to share my faith with gym users and staff members. Most of the time, I could push past embarrassment or my fear of rejection or ridicule. Sometimes people were open for conversation and even prayer. Other times they just laughed at me. Either way, I learnt that my purpose wasn't to get someone saved. It was to be obedient to the guidance of the Holy Spirit—to sense His

---

1. The Engle Scale of Evangelism, Outreach Magazine.

Presence guiding me to different people and to see what He wanted to do through me, always ensuring the person felt loved and honoured.

One story that stood out to me during this time was the parable of the sower, mentioned in Matthew 13:1–23. I was called to sow God's word into people's lives every day. Sometimes that seed fell on bad soil, and sometimes it fell on good soil. Either way, I was called to plant the seed of God's word. For the better part of ten months, I shared my faith in Jesus and my life with one of the gym managers. At first, he simply respected that I had a belief in Jesus. After some time, he began to understand my belief in Jesus meant we lived different lives and valued things differently. About six months into our friendship, his wife became rather ill. Through this ordeal, she began to pray and then attended an Alpha course.[2] This led her to attend church and start her own relationship with Jesus. He told me that going to church with his wife was helpful, as it gave him a moment to stop, think, and simply *be* rather than always *do*. Our conversations never got him any closer to embracing the Good News of Jesus. After twelve months of working there and ten months of sharing my life with him, I left that job to set up my own personal training business. I was disappointed that he was never willing to open his heart to Jesus and sad because I knew how much Jesus loved him.

We kept in contact here and there, and he was later promoted to club manager at a more prestigious gym in central London. Sometime after that, we met for coffee, and he told me that not only had he given his life to Jesus, but he was now serving the youth ministry.

---

2. Visit https://alpha.org

When I'd left the job at the gym, I thought this man was the seed that was thrown on the path. Every time I sowed the message of Jesus, the enemy was there to snatch it up. It turned out he was more like the seed thrown on good soil that produced a crop that was thirty, sixty, a hundred times more than what was sown. I was looking for instant growth—a speedy process of sowing, growing, and fruitfulness. God was leading this man through that process but was willing for it to take years. Looking back over our shared story, it's obvious to me that he journeyed from a −7 all the way to at least a +4 on the Engle scale. At the same time, he started asking me questions that peeled back layers of pain I'd held on to from people who'd laughed at me for my beliefs. God brought healing to both of our hearts during this time.

My concept of evangelism was once very binary—either someone got saved or they didn't. Over the years of sharing the Gospel with people, I moved away from that understanding and began to see my job as moving people along a scale like this.

This understanding has been very helpful. Sometimes I'm moving someone from a −7 to a −6, and at other times it's from a +3 to a +4. Both have value. We tend to think of evangelism as only covering −1 to 0, which is unhelpful and disempowers us. Every step matters. Some of us are better at certain steps than others, but every step counts. This book is aimed at those between −4 and +4 on the scale. I'm not here to convince you that God or the Gospel are real, but I do want to inspire and equip you to live more faithfully for Jesus.

Listening to Understand, Not to Respond

What does a −7 to −4 story look like? Well, a few weeks ago I was having a cup of tea with some elderly people in a local village. One of our church members has been gathering a small group of people in a sheltered accommodation near our church for some time. It's not a Bible study group or anything like that, just people in the same space hanging out. I'd come to visit because of a tragedy that had happened in that accommodation block a few weeks prior. A man had murdered two residents and then killed himself. There were maybe five of us, enjoying conversation and cake for a couple of hours. I got to talking with two of the older men. One seemed rather curious about faith and, in his own way, seemed to have a relationship with Jesus. The other was filled with pain but clothed it in the understanding that science had disproved Genesis 1–3, the creation narrative. Consequently, the rest of the Bible was a philosophy and was neither more or less true than any other historical philosophy, according to him.

One thing I've learnt over the years is to listen—and I mean really listen. Often, what people say and why they say it are not the same. As I've already said, this man was covering his pain with a view that science had disproven God. I could have debated the Gospel and Genesis with him, but he had a hurting heart that needed Jesus, not a brain that needed convincing of truth and explanation. As disciples, we can be so quick to perform Christian activity that we don't listen to people's hearts or feelings.

As I took time to understand this man's heart and listen beyond his words, the opportunity came to share God's love with him, and I believe he moved from a −7 to a −4 in that encounter. God was at work, and God will draw him into His Kingdom. I just simply played my part in God's plan, helping him to move along the Engle scale.

While working as a freelance personal trainer, one of my clients was the global director of a worldwide accountancy firm. He was a very wealthy, influential, and powerful man. He had no faith in God, but he didn't call himself an atheist either. He often insulted my beliefs, especially considering I didn't value material possessions the same way he did. During our sessions, I found it extremely challenging to talk to him about Jesus because this man could have anything he wanted whenever he wanted. I'd love to say that the situation eventually turned around, but it never did. Although I listened well and engaged with him, he stayed at a −7 on the scale. I felt like I had failed to share the wonder of living for and believing in Jesus in a way that spoke to his soul.

After one particular session in which he was rather unkind, I asked the Father about this. I felt God speak directly to me to remind me that one day everyone would account for their life on earth. When he stands before the Lord and God asks why he didn't believe in Jesus, the man will say no one told him. God will then say, "Didn't my servant Dave tell you of me?"

This was a profound moment for me. I learnt my role is really to share the message, and what people choose to do with it is up to them. We are released from that burden. Praise God!

Focusing on Love and Honour

As a church pastor, I'm aware that I can force a conversation about Jesus. This typically happens when I meet a new person and ask them what they do for a living. They are likely to ask me the same question, which opens the door for the Jesus conversation. Sometimes our motivation for sharing Jesus doesn't have anything to do with love and honour but rather comes from our own need to feel like we've performed. This really isn't healthy. We don't need to perform for God's approval. He already loves us. We are saved by God's grace, not our own efforts.

While on holiday, my wife and I befriended another vacationing family. For whatever reason, I felt compelled not to ask John what he did, hopefully ensuring he wouldn't ask me either. For five days, we managed to avoid talking about our jobs. The day they were supposed to leave, the Holy Spirit let me know it was time. I asked John what he did for a job, then he asked me what I did. When I told him, he followed up with, "So what does that mean you actually do?"

I gave him a rough outline of the role of a pastor. Then I told him I'd often spend a whole summer researching one topic to gain a better understanding about how the Bible and our modern lives line up. I explained I was currently studying Genesis 1 and 2 and the creation narrative. This fascinated him, and I proceeded to share about ancient cosmology. Often discussion based on Genesis 1 and 2 focuses on how they can be interpreted based on current scientific theories or research. This can sometimes be helpful, but a much better question to ask when reading the Bible is, who was the author's original audience? How did that audience understand the text?

In the case of Genesis 1 and 2, the audience would have known three predominant creation stories: one from Babylon, one from Egypt, and one from a people group called the Amorites. The stories are different but share common themes, such as multiple gods being involved in the process and some sort of battle with chaos or darkness. In contrast to these creation stories, Genesis 1 and 2 present one God speaking creation into being rather than many gods, and there is no great battle.[3]

We discussed ancient cosmology further, which enabled John to move past some of his objections to Christianity and faith in Jesus. That day, John moved from maybe a −4 to a −2. God was at work, calling another son home. I felt that I'd honoured the fact that we were both on holiday and didn't force a Gospel conversation upon him. Because we had this conversation near the end of the holiday rather than the beginning, John was far more open to it. He felt honoured rather than being the target of some overzealous Christian need to evangelise.

Simple Tips for Sharing Jesus

- Listen to what people are saying. If they share a problem with you, ask if you can pray for them.

- Actions matter. If people know you follow Jesus but you don't love and serve others, your actions won't match your faith. Be a living example of Jesus's teachings.

- Work on sharing your story succinctly.

- Talk more about Jesus than church. You are a follower of Jesus, not a follower of a church.

- Rather than inviting people to a church service, ask them if they'd like to study the Bible with you in a place they're more comfortable, such as a coffee shop, pub, or someone's home.

---

3. For more on Genesis, read The Geneological Adam and Eve: The Surprising Science of Universal Ancestry: /.

- Pray for opportunities to share about Jesus with others.

Feeling embarrassed, ill-equipped, awkward, or overly zealous is common among those who love Jesus and want to share their faith with others. You can overcome those feelings by shifting your focus to the scale of evangelism so it's less black and white. Listen well and practice love and honour. If the person you speak to walks away from the conversation feeling loved, that's great! Ultimately it's God who will draw people to Jesus, not us.

Prayer

Jesus, give me opportunities to share my faith. I ask that You help me overcome my fears and be led by Your Spirit to share Your love and goodness with my family, friends, and work colleagues. Amen.

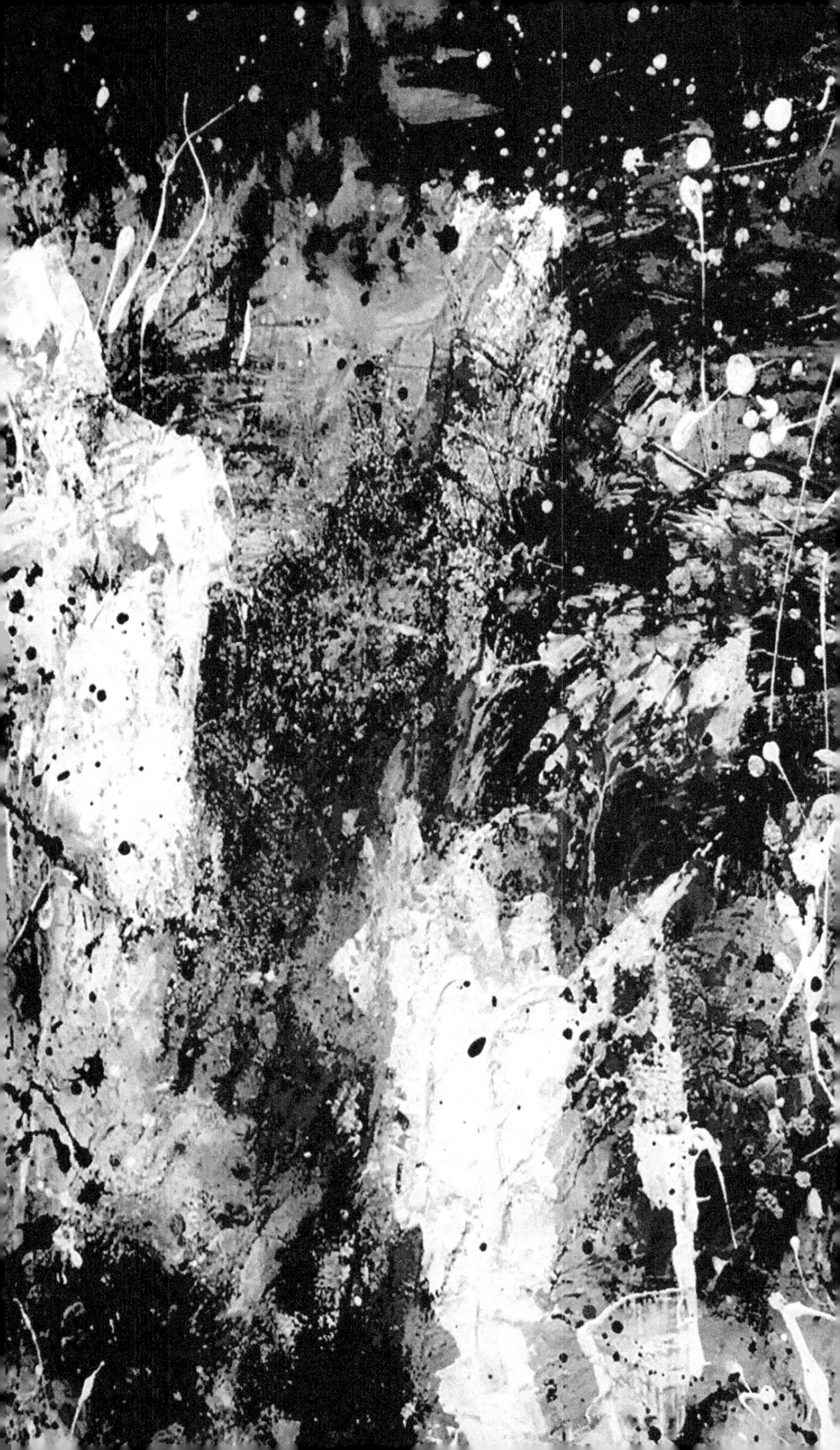

Chapter 11

Kingdom Jigsaw

While working as a personal trainer in Crouch End, I worked with Rachel, for whom the Holy Spirit gave me real compassion. Although she never said anything about it, her life was clearly filled with pain. I'd often pick her up on my way to work or drop her home afterwards if we were working the same shifts. Rachel would often comment about how kind I was, so for the better part of the year, I simply showed her kindness through these rides. Hardly the most overt sharing of the Gospel; literally anyone with a car could do this.

A year or so later, a few friends and I moved to the Grahame Park Estate. During our time of serving the community and sharing about Jesus, we saw a number of those struggling with addictions come to faith and, in some cases, really clean their lives up (such as Speedy, who I mentioned in a previous chapter). Another one of those people was an older guy named Dean. At first Dean wasn't interested in Jesus or church (he was at least a −5 on the Engle scale), but over time and through our pastor's love for him, his heart softened. We regularly talked about Jesus, and he eventually became a follower and part of our church family. I even had the privilege of baptising him.

Dean was a fun guy to have around. He was such a character and well known on the estate. He passed away in 2016, and it was at his funeral that I first saw the jigsaw puzzle of God's incredible Kingdom. I sat near the back with a few others from our church, but who was sitting right in front with the grieving family? Yes, you guessed it: Rachel!

After the service, I went over to her and asked how she knew Dean. It turned out Dean was her father. Once, he'd been a successful builder, but the business had struggled, he'd turned to alcohol, and the family had fallen apart. Rachel and Dean had some contact with each other, but she'd grown up with her mum and siblings while Dean's life was destroyed by addiction. Rachel had heard that Dean's life had been turned around in recent years through an encounter with Jesus and a local church community. Rachel had had no idea I was part of that church community, and I'd had no idea Dean and Rachel were related. I'd not seen her since starting my own personal training business many years before.

Rachel expressed her deepest gratitude to me for loving and caring for Dean. Since becoming a disciple of Jesus, he'd worked on his relationship with his family, and a measure of healing and restoration had taken place. It wasn't perfect, not by a long shot, but it was better than before. Rachel was grateful for the few years she could connect with Dean in a healthier way.

As I left the funeral that day, my mind was well and truly blown. I'd spent just under a year being kind to Rachel and about seven years loving Dean and aiding in his journey of faith. God was at work in both their lives, and I had no idea. He truly is awesome!

At the beginning of this book, I wrote about our lives being much like a jigsaw puzzle that the Father is putting together according to His plan. This story is but one example of the pieces of God's plan coming together. But let me offer another one.

Rescuer to Rescued

It was Remembrance Day. My family and I were living in Barnet, North London, and I was working for the Community Church. The journey to work was forty-five minutes on a good day—or hours if the M25 was packed with traffic. This day would turn out to be one of the most powerful in my life, and it created a memory my children are unlikely to forget.

After a fantastic Remembrance Service with the whole community on the Green, I jumped into the car with my two eldest kids. Kaz was at home with our youngest. The car wouldn't start, so I called the AA to pick us up and tow our car back to North London. When the recovery driver came, I knew God was up to something. His name was Lloyd, and he was covered in tattoos and clearly went to the gym. We got talking, and as we took the long journey around the M25, there was time to hear his story and heart. My children watched as I shared the Gospel with him. That day, Lloyd physically rescued us, but Jesus spiritually rescued him.

We exchanged numbers, and I encouraged him to read the Bible using the You Version app. Lloyd wasn't that conventional; he seemed to have journeyed with Jesus alone before attending church. Over the next five years, he grew astronomically in his faith. Although I had the privilege of leading Lloyd to Jesus, he's been part of several different church communities, as his work commitments moved him from place to place. We've stayed in touch, and I've cheered him on from the sidelines—and occasionally, when he's asked, spoken into his life.

As I write this, Lloyd has recently finished his second year of Bible college. He has become a fearless evangelist and has personally led hundreds of people to faith in Jesus through everyday interactions like the one we shared in his truck some years ago. Only God can do this kind of stuff, interweaving people's lives in such a mysteriously brilliant way.

Seed, Sapling, Tree

As we draw this book to a close, I hope it has inspired you to live an obedient life of adventurous authenticity with Jesus. One filled with mountaintop moments in which you see firsthand the Kingdom of God breaking into your ordinary life. A life as a disciple of Jesus in which you partner with the Holy Spirit to see the works of the devil destroyed and the kingdom of darkness pushed back, never getting stuck in the Valley of Ono.

These things don't tend to happen overnight. We need to persevere, demonstrate grit, and work through the grime. There are no shortcuts to Kingdom growth. All of Jesus's stories that talk of growth in God's Kingdom never indicate an instant effect, but a natural one. Each of these types of growth takes time. The mustard seed that becomes a plant then takes decades to become a tree, which can sustain the lives of other birds and insects.[1]

As disciples of Jesus, we need to learn the art of celebrating growth in every season, not just the final product. Celebrations help us recognise what God has done and is doing, stop us from being distracted, and provide moments of fun. If life in the Kingdom were one of consistent growth and fruitfulness, Jesus wouldn't have taught us about the vine in John 15. Life as a disciple of Jesus has seasons of planting, growth,

---

1. See Luke 13:19.

fruitfulness, and pruning. There are even seasons of death, which lead to multiplication when the seeds fall to the ground.

We should develop a more rounded perspective on growth, one that embraces all the aforementioned seasons, but especially pruning and death. God is the Alpha (the Starter) and the Omega (the Finisher) of all things.

The Gospel Is Enough

Living out the Gospel of Jesus in your everyday life is the best way to demonstrate the Kingdom of God on Earth. It's what enables us to go into the world and make disciples as Jesus instructed.

The ways of Jesus do not need to compromise with worldly standards to stay relevant; life in the Kingdom doesn't need spicing up.

The Gospel of Jesus and His Kingdom are all we need in every way!

We are called to be beautifully intolerant of the ways of this world. We are called to be *in* the world not *of* the world, to love God the Father, Son, and Holy Spirit, and live lives that bring forth incredible glory to God, through grit and grime. As the apostle Paul says, "Live a life worthy of the Lord and please Him in every way: bearing fruit in every good work, growing in the knowledge of God" (Colossians 1:10).

I pray that you'll have tonnes of fun with Jesus and see God's glory fulfil your dreams. The best is yet to come, and one day we're going to party in Heaven, where there will be no more sickness, pain, distress, or even death. But until that day, let's keep returning to the Garden of Gethsemane and praying as Jesus did in Luke 22:44:

If it is possible, may this cup be taken from Me. Yet not as I will, but as You will.

About the Author

DAVE PRICE GREW UP in a Christian home but strayed from the faith of his parents until personal circumstance and divine intervention led him to a place of personal faith and conviction. Through various trials and victories, Dave's faith in Jesus has grown, and now he wants to help others make sense of life's ups and downs, demonstrating that an authentic faith in Jesus is the best way to live. You can contact Dave at info@jesusmovement.live

For more resources visit
www.jesusmovement.live/resources

Printed in Great Britain
by Amazon